Harnessing the Power of
Signs & Symbols

Harnessing the Power of

Signs & Symbols

UNLOCK THE SECRETS AND MEANINGS
OF THESE ANCIENT FIGURES

Kirsten Riddle

CICO BOOKS
LONDON NEW YORK

This edition published in 2022 by CICO Books
An imprint of Ryland Peters & Small Ltd
20–21 Jockey's Fields   341 E 116th St
London WC1R 4BW   New York, NY 10029

www.rylandpeters.com

10 9 8 7 6 5 4 3 2 1

First published in 2015 as *Discovering Signs & Symbols*

A CIP catalog record for this book is available from the Library of Congress and the British Library.

ISBN: 978 1 80065 089 3

Printed in China

Editor: Jennifer Jahn
Designer: Emily Breen
Illustrator: Dionne Kitching

Art director: Sally Powell
Production manager: Gordana Simakovic
Publishing manager: Penny Craig
Publisher: Cindy Richards

CONTENTS

THE POWER OF
SIGNS & SYMBOLS

The world is made up of signs and symbols. They are inescapably entwined with all of creation. You only have to look to the landscape to see and feel their presence, from the stars that litter the night sky to the shining orb of the moon and its many different phases. The earth itself, the shape of a globe, is a circle that represents completion.

Symbols and patterns are all around us. They are inherent to who we are, binding us together, and providing a sense of unity and completion. They give us an insight into cultural history, helping us understand the past, where we came from, and who we are today. They help us see the magic in our everyday existence. Most importantly, we connect to them on a spiritual level, because they trigger our subconscious mind and generate self-awareness and power that we can use to transform any area of life. Even simple symbols based on shapes that we see on a daily basis can become powerful tools that help us manifest the things we want.

Consider the equilateral triangle, a shape made up of three sides of identical length: a symbol of unity, of three elements perfectly balanced and never-ending, like the past, the present, and the future. So easy to draw, it is no wonder the Celts used it in their knot-work designs, basing the Triskele, a famous symbol made up of three spiraling legs, upon its structure. To them it represented movement, a timeless progression like the cycle of life, from birth to death and then rebirth.

With this in mind, it is easy to see why arrows are often depicted with a triangular head, because they are pointing into the future, showing the way forward with balance and strength. Consciously, we might not pick up on this, but on a deeper level we connect with the triangle and understand its symbolism. The only way is up, like the triangular pyramids, the pinnacles of which point to the sun and capture its rays. So if we want to move forward in life and achieve our goals, then focusing on the triangle can help. Harnessing its power by bringing it to mind and seeing it as a tool to clear the path to success is all it takes. Whether you choose to draw it or picture it in a short visualization, it will put you in the right frame of mind to fulfill your dreams.

Our ancestors understood the power of signs and symbols. They embraced this energy, creating wonderful stories to explain their presence, but also took this a step further, using symbols in rituals and ceremonial worship. From the feisty Norse gods and their symbols of strength and power, such as Thor's hammer, to the mystical Egyptians, always searching for a deeper meaning with talismans, such as the Ankh or the Eye of Horus. Every mythology has a richly woven folklore that uses signs and symbols as the basis for magical workings. These symbols have survived because they have become embedded into our psyche. Over time, they have grown into archetypes with which we associate and that we can use in a number of ways.

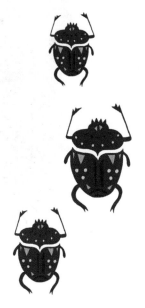

Today, we're surrounded by these symbols. We might not always notice them, but they are here, in the fabric of society. They turn up in the most unexpected places, such as the famous restaurant chain whose giant "M" sign—made up of two golden arches—represents a portal into another world of eating and pleasure (golden arches often appeared in folklore to represent transition into another dimension). It is no accident that Mickey Mouse has such a large, round head and round ears. His shape was based on a number of circles, because circles are considered safe by small children. Even at a young age we identify circular structures with a sense of wholeness and security.

The language of signs and symbols is easy to understand once you get started. As you read this book and dig deeper, you will find that you not only identify with the folklore, but you will begin to make it personal. You will connect with certain shapes and symbols and feel a pull toward them. They will arouse feelings and emotions that will affect your attitude and behavior. You will pay attention to them in your life and harness their power. This is because they engage your intuition. As you are working with them, you will find that your sixth sense takes over and you intuit things on a number of levels. You might even feel the need to create your own signs and symbols to use in different areas of your life, by combining examples from mythologies or coming up with your own designs, for example.

Working with signs and symbols is a personal journey, and it is up to you how and when you use them. Each chapter in this book covers a different mythology, looking at the origins and folklore of some of the most powerful symbols and offering tips and rituals that you can use to tap into their energy. You can adapt any of the rituals or create your own using the suggestions as a guide. You may feel drawn to a particular mythology and want to focus solely on that area, or you may want to search for signs and symbols that can help you in a specific area of your life, for example with love, money, or health. It is entirely up to you. Working with signs and symbols can be fascinating, fun, and extremely magical, so enjoy!

Getting Started

You do not need any special equipment or tools to get started, just an open mind and heart and a sense of adventure. But to get the most out of the experience, there are some practical steps that you can take.

Invest in a notebook and turn it into a journal of all the signs and symbols that you are interested in. Use it to record the ones you like, as well as any thoughts, feelings, or impressions you get from them. You can also use it to reflect on any of the activities or rituals that you try in this book. As you work with signs and symbols, you may start to notice their appearance in other areas of your life. You might notice coincidences as you go about your everyday routines or have symbolic dreams, so make some space to record these experiences. They might not make much sense at first, but over time you might see a pattern of symbols emerging that could be pointing you in a specific direction or providing an insight into the future. For example, you might be drawn to symbols associated with the moon and, as you explore this further, you might find that you're interested in moon magic, or you might want to develop your intuitive and psychic skills, also associated with the moon.

Create some space in your home to incorporate important signs and symbols into your life. You might want to dedicate a corner of your living room to your favorites or make some space on a table or shelf. Fill this area with symbols that you are drawn to or use it for a particular aim, such as attracting good fortune, money, or love.

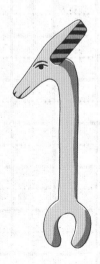

Although you can work with signs and symbols anytime and anywhere, it is useful to allocate a regular time slot every week for this purpose. Make sure you will not be disturbed and, to make it special, mark out some sacred space by lighting candles and burning essential oils that promote relaxation and psychic development, such as lavender and rosemary. Use this time to develop your intuition and carry out symbolic rituals or to catch up on some research into your favorite signs and symbols.

YOUR SIGNS & SYMBOLS

To help you get started and discover to which particular group of symbols you are most drawn, try this easy quiz.

1 In a spiritual bookshop, what kind of books are you drawn to?
- [ ] **A** Books on different types of faith
- [ ] **B** Books on earth magic and the elements
- [ ] **C** Ancient scriptures
- [ ] **D** Books on gods and goddesses
- [ ] **E** Tales about magical creatures
- [ ] **F** Books on voodoo and magic around the world

2 What's your favorite type of movie?
- [ ] **A** Vampire and werewolf movies
- [ ] **B** Movies about sorcerers
- [ ] **C** Historical movies with plenty of battle scenes
- [ ] **D** Mythical movies with lots of folklore
- [ ] **E** Movies with a seafaring, nautical theme
- [ ] **F** Movies in exotic locations with great scenery

3 Friends would describe you as:
- [ ] **A** Intriguing and mysterious
- [ ] **B** Nature loving and creative
- [ ] **C** Indulgent and vivacious
- [ ] **D** Fun loving and passionate
- [ ] **E** Assertive and clever
- [ ] **F** Grounded and magical

4 You would describe your dress sense as:
- [ ] **A** Quirky and unique
- [ ] **B** Floaty and feminine
- [ ] **C** Extravagant with lots of wonderful fabrics
- [ ] **D** Designer all the way
- [ ] **E** Practical and sassy
- [ ] **F** Vibrant with lots of eye-catching prints

5 To relax, which of the following would you choose to do?
- [ ] **A** Spend some time in quiet reflection
- [ ] **B** Go for a walk in the countryside
- [ ] **C** Visit a spa for some pampering
- [ ] **D** Take a long, luxurious bath
- [ ] **E** Go for a run
- [ ] **F** Put on your favorite track and dance

6 What kind of music do you like?
- [ ] **A** Traditional tunes with a modern edge
- [ ] **B** Celtic folk music
- [ ] **C** Fast exotic beats that get you dancing
- [ ] **D** Funky pop music
- [ ] **E** Rock anthems
- [ ] **F** Tribal chants and rhythms

7 If you had a magic power it would be:
- [ ] **A** To predict the future
- [ ] **B** To heal
- [ ] **C** To travel to other worlds
- [ ] **D** To manifest anything
- [ ] **E** To be incredibly strong
- [ ] **F** To shape shift

8 If you could travel anywhere in the world, which of the following options would you choose?
- [ ] **A** An adventure in Romania
- [ ] **B** Walking in the Scottish Highlands
- [ ] **C** A cruise down the Nile
- [ ] **D** A city break in Rome
- [ ] **E** A trip down the Fjords
- [ ] **F** An African safari

9 In a museum, what would you look at first?
- [ ] **A** Anything dark and mysterious, such as funeral objects
- [ ] **B** Sacred, carved objects used in rituals
- [ ] **C** Ornate and decorative jewelry
- [ ] **D** Beautiful tiles and statues
- [ ] **E** Stone carvings and weaponry
- [ ] **F** Tribal weapons and clothing

RESULTS

Read the explanations below to find out which type of symbols you are likely to be drawn to, then turn to the chapter to find out more.

Mostly As

If you chose mostly As, then you are drawn to the magic and mystery of the ancient Slavic people. You like their sense of majesty and you will be interested to learn about their beliefs and traditions. Like them, you are drawn to the quirky side of life. You like to unravel mysteries and spend a lot of time in meditation. The religious side of these signs and symbols will intrigue you, and you will love learning about their sacred practices and how you can tap into their power today.

Mostly Bs

You are rooted in nature and Mother Earth and, if you chose mostly Bs, then you have a natural affinity with the Celts and their way of life. You love being outside and you are attuned to the environment. You are fascinated by wildlife, and, in particular, you like to visit sacred spots. You will identify with some of the intricate designs used in Celtic symbols, and you will enjoy deciphering each layer of the pattern and what it represents. Fascinated by magic and mystery, you will understand the deeper workings of the signs and symbols of this mythology.

Mostly Cs

If you chose mostly Cs, then the intriguing rituals of the ancient Egyptians will appeal to you, as well as the way they used signs and symbols in their clothing and to decorate temples. Like them, you are a passionate and mysterious soul, fascinated by other worlds. Life's mysteries intrigue you, and you will enjoy reading about the symbols that were important to the ancient Egyptians and how they used them in magical ceremonies.

Mostly Ds

Like the pleasure-seeking Greeks and Romans, you enjoy all the best things in life. You like to indulge and appreciate art and beauty, and so you will identify with the way they used signs and symbols to appeal to the gods and to decorate their homes. You will enjoy reading up on the myths and legends associated with these symbols and learning how to use them today, to manifest the things you want. A natural leader, you will be particularly interested in creating your own power symbol that you can use in any area of your life.

Mostly Es

Like the fiery Norse warriors of old, you are feisty and assertive. You naturally identify with their way of life because you enjoy a challenge. Confident and charming, you find it easy to think on your feet. With you, it is about practicality, and you will appreciate the efficient nature of some of the Norse signs and symbols. You will enjoy re-living some of the epic battles associated with the Norse people. In particular, you will enjoy re-creating some of the symbols and applying them to problem areas in your life.

Mostly Fs

If you chose mostly Fs, then you are drawn to the mystical influences of Africa. You appreciate the wisdom of its ancient tribes. Like them, you will find that you are connected to the natural world and to the rhythms of the earth. You are fascinated by tales of shamans, and you appreciate the power of other creatures. You will enjoy reading up on the folk tales associated with the symbols and learning how to create your own sacred rituals to harness their power.

Celtic Signs
& Symbols

Celtic mythology is littered with signs and symbols—from intricate knot-work designs to stone carvings and ancient monuments that dominate the landscape in the United Kingdom and Ireland. It is easy to feel a Celtic presence in our surroundings. Indeed, some of the more popular symbols appear in our everyday lives, in jewelry and fashion, and as symbols that we still work with. The Triskele, for example, has been adopted in practical signs—it is used, for example, in the seal of the US Department of Transportation and the badge of the Victoria Highlanders, the Canadian soccer team. Despite this popularity, many of the Celtic beliefs and traditions associated with these symbols have been lost over time. However, we can still connect to the power of these symbols by developing a personal relationship with them and learning to think like our Celtic ancestors.

AILM

(OL-UM)

This ancient Celtic symbol stands for purity and is the 20th letter of the Ogham alphabet—an early medieval alphabet that was used to form the ancient Irish language. The circle around the symbol represents wholeness and a sense of completion; it also symbolizes a balanced and intact soul. The cross in the center of the circle represents the branches of the fir tree, one of the nine sacred trees used in druid tradition for making ceremonial fires and which—because of the way it stands, straight and tall—is associated with longevity, strength, and endurance. The Ailm is simple to draw on, or carve into, the bark of trees. It has a long association with honesty, clarity, and good health, because fir trees remain green and strong throughout the year—a sign of their resilient nature. If you are lacking in stamina or motivation, the Ailm symbol can help. Tap into its power to boost health and well-being.

AILM *Ritual*

If you are feeling low and in need of a boost, connect to the power of Mother Nature with this Ailm ritual. Find a quiet spot outside where you will not be disturbed, if possible, near a tree. Take a stick and draw a large circle in the earth. Stand in the center of the circle and draw a cross. Position yourself at the central point of the cross. Feel your weight drop down into your feet and let yourself bounce lightly up and down for a minute. Notice how the earth supports you. Breathe in and connect to the power of the Ailm; feel its pure, white energy surging through your body. Breathe out and imagine releasing all your worries and fears. Spend a few minutes tapping into the energy of the Ailm. You should begin to feel more energized and at peace. Finally, take a piece of quartz crystal and imagine condensing that feeling of inner strength into the crystal by pouring your outward breath into it. Keep the crystal with you as a reminder of the Ailm symbol and its powerful gift.

Magical Tip

For clarity and insight, burn pine-scented oil and carry a sprig from a fir tree in your pocket.

AWEN

(AH-WHEN)

In Welsh, the word Awen means poetic inspiration. The symbol represents the primordial breath of light from the gods that inspires us and ignites the fire within. It is a sign of spiritual illumination and often referred to as the Three Rays of Light. The left and right rays symbolize the male and female aspects of the spirit, and the central ray represents the balance between the two. Used as a glyph in modern druidism, Awen is often associated with the Welsh goddess Ceridwen and her cauldron of wisdom. It was thought that if you drank from this cauldron, you'd be given the gift of Awen. Some druids believe that the three rays of light in the symbol represent the sunrise at midsummer, which casts three spreading rays that open the doorway into the Celtic otherworld. Use this symbol to gain wisdom and knowledge and to unleash your creative spirit on the world.

Magical Tip

To get your creative juices flowing, light three gold candles to represent the three rays of light of the Awen. Grab a pen and paper and write down the first three words you can think of, then try and connect them to form a poem.

AWEN *Ritual*

Boost your brainpower and connect with your inner sage with this inspiring ritual.

Take a small bowl of warm water to represent Ceridwen's cauldron and add to this three drops of lavender essential oil, to represent the Awen. With a towel over your head, lean over the bowl and breathe deeply for three or four minutes. Close your eyes and let any thoughts, images, or words appear. Ask the Awen to bless you with wisdom and psychic skills. When you are ready, remove the towel, take the bowl of water, and offer it up to the sun by casting it outside. Alternatively, if you prefer to carry this ritual out at night, soak a flannel in the remaining water, drain it of any excess liquid, and then place over your forehead to soothe you into sleep and promote prophetic dreams.

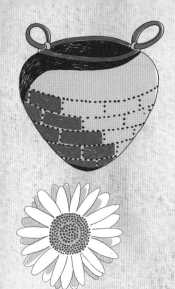

CAULDRON

At the heart of every Celtic home was the Cauldron. Used for cooking, brewing, and also in magical rituals for divination, the Cauldron is associated with the element of water and was often thrown into rivers and streams as a sacrifice to the gods. The Celts believed the ocean was one big Cauldron of divine inspiration, and so the sea is often linked to poets and bards who would draw their artistic gifts from this universal pot. The Dagda, a mythical fairy race thought to be the ancestors of the Celts, owned the Cauldron of Plenty, which provided a never-ending supply of food and drink. In the otherworld, the Cauldron was often associated with deities, the most famous being the Goddess of wisdom, Ceridwen. The powers of this cooking pot were renowned and, over time, as the church's influence spread, it became associated with Christ's holy cup and also the Holy Grail. Tap into the power of this ancient symbol to increase wisdom and to attract a wealth of abundance and prosperity.

The Cauldron is associated with the element of water and was often thrown into rivers and streams as a sacrifice to the gods.

CAULDRON *Ritual*

Clear your mind and boost intelligence with this reviving ritual. Find a place outside with flowing water, such as a river, stream, or a well. Alternatively, run a bath of warm water and stand before it. Hold a white flower in your hands to represent your connection to nature and the divine Cauldron of inspiration. Say, "May inspiration flower, may wisdom grow strong. May the seasons ebb and flow, as life moves on." Toss the flower into the water and then say, "Cauldron of divine inspiration, bless me with insight." Spend a few moments thinking about the way the water moves and how every ripple is connected. Imagine standing beneath a fountain of light, which cleanses you from head to toe.

Magical Tip

To increase the flow of prosperity in your life, picture a giant gold Cauldron. Imagine dipping your hands into its depths and pulling out an abundance of treasure. If you have something specific in mind, for example a new car, see that emerging from the Cauldron of Plenty.

CELTIC CROSS

A symbol of hope, faith, and balance, the Celtic Cross can be interpreted in many different ways. The center of the Cross is pivotal; it is the power point from which we can re-focus, recharge, and gain insight. The Celts believed that this was the source of divine energy, with each arm representing a branch of wisdom and a different path. On a practical level, the four arms of the Cross could represent the four Celtic fire festivals (Samhain, Imbolc, Beltane, Lughnasadh). Each of these festivals marked the passing of time and a different cycle of the seasons, and therefore the Cross is often associated with transition and the everlasting cycles of life. The ring around the center of the Cross has a number of meanings. It is thought that it represents the Roman solar deity, Sol Invictus, which explains the Cross's association with the sun. Another theory suggests that it is related to the halo of Christ. If you are seeking clarity, spiritual insight, or the courage to face your fears, the Celtic Cross symbol can help.

Magical Tip

For protection and strength on the go, imagine carrying a shield emblazoned with the Celtic Cross. Any negative energy will instantly rebound from the shield, leaving you protected from head to toe.

CELTIC CROSS *Ritual*

Create a Celtic Cross altar where you can charge your aura and boost
personal power. Find a space in your home, preferably somewhere
bathed in natural light coming from
a window, and fill it with objects and
images that capture the spirit of the
Cross. For example, you might have
pictures or symbols that you have
drawn or stones that remind you of its
shape. Pictures of the sun are also
helpful as they represent the solar
influence and the changing seasons.
Every day, light a candle and spend
some time in the presence of your altar.
Close your eyes and visualize yourself
sitting beneath a giant Celtic Cross.
Feel it strengthening your inner core and
showering you with power and love.
Know that you are protected in this
space, while you replenish your
spiritual energy.

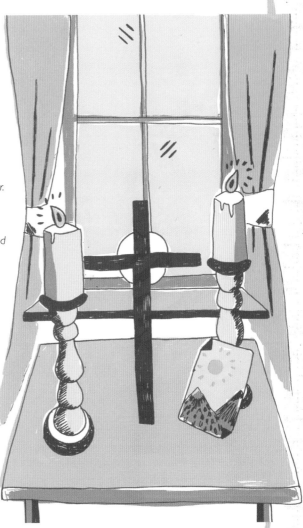

FIVE FOLD SYMBOL

One of the most complex of all Celtic symbols, the Five Fold Symbol comprises five interlocking circles, the fifth of which is situated in the center, representing the fifth element. The first four circles represent different aspects that fit together neatly to make a whole, for example, spring, summer, fall, and winter, which make up the wheel of the year, or the four elements of earth, air, fire, and water. The fifth element is created when the other four come together; it is the central focus of all power, the divine essence that gives life to everything. The druids believed this symbol to be highly sacred as it represents a unified energy and a balance among all things. Some experts suggest that the central circle symbolizes the universe and that the Five Fold Symbol is a statement about human nature. Work with this symbol to boost personal power and enhance your sixth sense.

The fifth element is created when the other four come together; it is the central focus of all power, the divine essence that gives life to everything.

FIVE FOLD *Ritual*

To heal a broken heart and help you release past hurts, try this
Five Fold ritual. Clear a table and place four crystals in each
corner to represent the four elements of the Five Fold
symbol. In the center of the table, place a white candle
to represent the fifth element, which brings everything
together. Start by imagining a thread of light
extending up and toward the tip of the candle from
each of the four crystals. Imagine these threads
meeting to ignite the flame. Take a deep breath and
light the candle. Say, "Divine power wash over me.
Help me find balance and serenity. Light the flame
and heal my heart. Help me make a fresh start."
Imagine standing in the center of a sphere of light, feel
yourself connected and replenished by the universe. Repeat
the magical affirmation and let the candle burn down naturally.

Magical Tip

Because the Five Fold symbol is based
on a series of circles, it is easy to draw
(with some practice). Have a go at creating
your own colorful mandala that you can
focus on while meditating to help you
tap into your higher self.

TREE OF LIFE

A symbol of harmony and balance, the Celtic people revered the Tree of Life. They believed that the Tree united the upper and lower worlds, as its roots spread deeply underground and its branches reached out to the heavens. This spirit of harmony and wholeness is embodied in the way trees work together to build a forest, sustaining one another, and providing a home for wildlife. The Celts believed that trees were magical beings that lived and breathed and could be used as doorways into the spirit world. They watched them change throughout the seasons, taking note of how they shed their leaves in the fall, only to be reborn again in the spring. As a result, the Tree of Life was also thought to symbolize renewal. Many Celtic knot-work designs show the Tree of Life encircled by its roots and branches, which join together to make a continuous loop.

TREE OF LIFE *Ritual*

Increase the joy in your life by taking inspiration from ancient traditions. The Celts would often pick one tree in a field to represent the Tree of Life and then honor it with gifts. Follow their lead and choose your own Tree of Life. Spend some time sitting beneath its branches. Imagine striking up a conversation with the spirit of the tree. You can do this in your head if you prefer. Share your thoughts, feelings, and worries. Tell it stories or use it as a place to share special memories. Take an offering along with you, something simple like a flower, crystal, or a poem that you have written, and leave it at the base of the tree. If you are looking to cement a relationship or friendship, spend some time together beneath the branches of the tree and let its harmonious energy bind you together.

Magical Tip

Celebrate the power of the Tree of Life by growing your own love tree. Sprinkle apple seeds in a pot filled with soil and water them while picturing yourself happy and in love.

TRIQUETRA

(TRAHY–KWE–TRUH)

One of many symbols based on the power of three, the Triquetra appears in Celtic knot-work and decoration, and can be found carved into ancient relics. It is usually linked to the triple goddess and her three aspects, the maiden, mother, and crone, and is also closely associated with the moon. Its triplicity can be interpreted as representing the past, present, and future; mind, body, and spirit; and father, mother, and child. Often associated with the goddess Brigid, who governed art, healing, and metal work, the Triquetra represents three elements working together in harmony. Sometimes this symbol appears surrounded by a circle, which is thought to represent eternal love and the continuing cycles of life. If you want to balance mind, body, and soul, and feel empowered, work with the Triquetra.

Its triplicity can be interpreted as representing the past, present, and future; mind, body, and spirit; and father, mother, and child.

TRIQUETRA *Ritual*

Honor the triple aspects of the goddess, and increase your personal power and confidence with this ritual. Take three candles, one small, one medium, and one large, to represent the maiden, mother, and crone aspects of the triple goddess. Sprinkle a mixture of salt and pepper (representing protection and strength) in a circle around the candles. Light the candles in order from smallest to largest (the lit candles represent eternal light and love) and hold an image of the Triquetra in your mind. If it helps, draw the symbol on a piece of paper and place it in front of the candles. Imagine standing in a giant Triquetra of fiery light. See yourself stepping between the three loops of the symbol as you connect with all three aspects of the goddess. As the candles burn down, spend some time contemplating the strengths of each persona. For example, the maiden has youth and beauty on her side, the mother is life-giving and nurturing, and the crone is wise. Remind yourself of these qualities within your own personality and make a positive statement, such as, "I embrace the triple aspects of my soul!"

Magical Tip

To maintain harmony in the work place, arrange items on your desk in groups of three like the Triquetra. For example, place three pen pots together or position files in staggered groups of three.

TRISKELE

(TRIS-KEEL)

This intricate design of three Celtic knots has many meanings. As its shape is wheel-like, it is often associated with movement and progression. The Triskele rolls forward into the future; it turns like the cycles of life and represents the never-ending change of the seasons. The legs of the Triskele are often associated with three inter-related elements, such as the past, present, and future. There are many different interpretations and that is part of Triskele's power. Most scholars agree that the Celts associated it with the three different worlds: the present, otherworld, and celestial world. It was also thought to have lunar connections, the three legs representing the three key phases of the moon. The Triskele is often worn to promote creativity, intuition, and psychic insights. To bring illumination to an area of your life, or for personal growth, tap into Triskele's energy.

TRISKELE *Ritual*

To make your dreams come true and manifest a positive future, try this powerful ritual. On a piece of paper, draw three circles in the shape of a triangle, one circle on top of the other two, which are positioned next to each other. This is a representation of the Triskele. Think of three areas of your life that you'd like to improve or three wishes that you would like to see come true. Write a word to sum up each area or wish in each circle. Beneath the word write three things you could do to help improve this area or to manifest your wish. As you write, imagine yourself doing each thing. Then fold the paper three times and say, "By the power vested in me and the power of three, I manifest my future perfectly!" Keep the paper somewhere safe and read it every day, repeating the magical chant.

Magical Tip

Use the power of three to carve an exciting future. Every morning, look in the mirror and repeat this affirmation three times while picturing the Triskele in your mind: "I move forward, I create, I innovate!"

Going Further

Much of the history and many facts relating to Celtic traditions have been lost or altered through the passage of time. The largely oral tradition of the Celts was eventually superseded by more advanced systems of recording beliefs and traditions. This means that if you want to learn more about Celtic signs and symbols, you have to do some legwork. The Celts were a spiritual race. They believed that the otherworld was real and not simply a supernatural realm a million miles away. To them, this other dimension was easy to access. They developed a personal relationship with the earth, and this extended to the symbols they used. To discover more, you need to develop a personal relationship with the signs and symbols listed in this chapter. Meditate on them. Create visualizations that you can use every day. Make them a part of your life. Get to know the power of the natural world and combine this with your knowledge of signs and symbols. Try the following top tips.

- Create a sacred space outside and get into the Celtic way of thinking. Find a corner of your garden—or just a flower planter if you do not have a lot of space—and use crystals and pretty stones to mark out the area. Plant your favorite flowers and herbs in this space. Alternatively, if you have a larger garden with a tree or a favorite spot in your local park, use this as your spiritual hot spot.

- Use your sacred space to connect with nature and meditate on the meaning of some of the symbols suggested in this chapter. Draw them in the soil or just sit, breathe deeply, and picture them in your mind.

- Recognize the power of the seasons and learn how to use this power to make the most of your magical rituals. By understanding the importance of nature, like the Celts, you will form a deeper connection with the signs and symbols that were inherent to their way of life.

Egyptian Signs & Symbols

The ancient Egyptians prized signs and symbols above all else and recognized their innate power. They created an entire language using signs, called hieroglyphs, to communicate their ideas. These glyphs, which numbered nearly 7,000, were often based on objects such as tools, and animals and birds, and although they represented sounds, they could have a number of meanings. They were called the Divine Word and seen as a gift from the god of writing, Thoth. Symbols were also used in the Egyptians' scriptures and pictures and carved into temple walls, pillars, and furnishings. Each of these symbols had a powerful meaning that could be used in magical rites and rituals. Sometimes the Egyptians would paint the symbol on their skin or create ornate jewels, which they would wear as talismans for protection and strength. Many of these symbols were associated with deities and used in petitions for magical help. Today we can tap into the magical power of the Egyptians by working with these signs and symbols and learning about their mystical associations.

ANKH

(ANGK)

This potent Egyptian symbol of a cross with a loop at the top represents eternal life. Also known as the Key of the Nile, it symbolizes the connection between the earth and the afterlife, and many Egyptian deities were pictured with the Ankh. It was thought that holding the Ankh meant that you had the power of life and death at your fingertips. Closely associated with the elixir of immortality, the Ankh was a life-giving tool, its perfect and continual loop representing the soul. It was also linked to water and that element's rejuvenating properties. Commonly used in funeral ceremonies and carved into the walls of tombs, the Ankh was often reversed so that it resembled a key, which the dead could then use to gain access to the afterlife. It was placed on the forehead of a dead person, between the eyes. In this position it was thought to guard any secrets. The goddess of life, death, and wisdom, Isis, is closely associated with the Ankh. Often considered to be the mother of all creation, she is linked with the fields where crops were grown, making her a nourishing, life-giving deity and so fit to carry this sacred symbol. For health, wealth, and an abundance of positive energy, work with the Ankh.

Magical Tip

To unlock good fortune, take an Ankh or a key to represent this sacred symbol and place it in a dish with a written request for prosperity. Every day, picture in your mind turning the key to a magical room that is filled with treasures.

ANKH *Ritual*

To help you on your path to success, try this easy ritual. Dip your finger into a few drops of sunflower oil—associated with the sun—and trace a large image of an Ankh onto a sheet of white paper. Inside the loop of the Ankh make a list of any problems or obstacles that are preventing you from moving forward in your life. Finally, light a white candle to represent the moon goddess Isis and pass the paper through the flame. Once it catches fire, let it burn to ashes in a fireproof bowl. Say, "I clear the path, I start anew. I clear the way for blessings true!" Scatter the ashes outside and repeat the magical chant. Be sure to visualize yourself happy, healthy, and prosperous.

EYE OF HORUS

One of the most powerful Egyptian symbols, the Eye of Horus has many names, including the All Seeing Eye and the Wedjat. The Eye represents the sun and symbolizes light, joy, and protection, and is associated with the sun god Horus, one of the oldest deities in the Egyptian pantheon. The Eye is often found on funerary objects because it is thought to light the path of the dead into the underworld. The teardrop below the eye is believed to match the markings around the eye of the falcon, which was associated with Horus. Other tales present the teardrop as a scar, left on Horus after a fight with Set, the god of the desert, storms, and disorder.

The spiral that stretches out below the eye represents a serpent, and signifies great wisdom and the changing cycles of life. The serpent is also often associated with movement and the continuing nature of life and death. The Eye of Horus is a powerful totem, commonly used in protection rituals. Harness the energy of this symbol whenever you need help to turn a corner or move on from a bad situation. The Eye of Horus will give you the power and strength you need to overcome obstacles in your path.

Magical Tip

Protect your home by copying an image of the Eye of Horus onto a piece of paper and placing it beneath a doormat near the entrance of your house.

EYE OF HORUS *Ritual*

Re-ignite your passion for life using the power of the Eye of Horus. At dawn, when the sun is rising, find a quiet spot and stand outside. Breathe deeply and tilt your face upward so that you can feel the first rays of sunlight. Trace the symbol of the Eye over your chest area, and imagine it's emblazoned with fire. Feel the warmth of the flames warm your heart. Open your arms wide and imagine embracing the sun. Say, "With the eye of Horus in my heart, I seek to make this fire start. The divine flame, it now burns bright and blesses me with love and light!" Repeat the chant three times, while continuing to trace the symbol of the eye on your chest. Take a few minutes to enjoy the life-giving energy of the sun as it showers you with blessings.

Feel the warmth of the flames warm your heart. Open your arms wide and imagine embracing the sun.

FEATHER OF MAAT

The Feather of Maat, which is associated with the goddess of justice and said to have been taken from her headdress, is a symbol of fairness and balance. It was thought that when someone died, that person was led into the Hall of Justice where he or she would have to face Osiris, the Lord of the Dead. At this point, the person's heart would be weighed on the scales of justice against the Feather of Maat. A good person's heart would weigh the same as the feather, but a bad person's would be heavier. Those who were deemed bad would die the eternal death, their heart being eaten by the goddess Ammut; but those who were good would go on to join the deities of eternal life. The Feather of Maat is a highly sacred symbol because Maat is one of the most powerful deities in the Egyptian pantheon.

Magical Tip

To cleanse your aura, the energy field around the body, take a feather and waft it around your silhouette, making short, sharp flicking movements to brush away any stagnant energy.

FEATHER OF MAAT *Ritual*

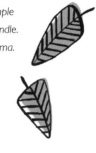

If you need help weighing up a problem or choosing a path, try this simple ritual. Take a pin and carve a feather shape into the wax of a white candle. Lightly trace your finger over the shape while thinking about your dilemma. Light the candle and spend a few minutes focusing on the feather shape. Speak your problem or question out loud, then close your eyes. Let any thoughts or images come to you; they may be insights that could help you. Let the candle burn down and make a note of any impressions you had. This ritual works particularly well before bedtime and can produce prophetic dreams.

SCARAB

The symbol of the Scarab was sacred to the ancient Egyptians and featured in their artwork, jewelry, and amulets. The Egyptians were fascinated by these beetles, which would lay their eggs in balls of dung and then roll the balls into the earth. The eggs would hatch and the young would feed and then emerge into the waiting sunlight. The Egyptians likened this process to the sun's daily journey, and they created a Scarab beetle god called Khepera, who—they believed—rolled the sun through the sky like a ball of dung. The emergence of the young beetles from their burrow seemed spontaneous and creative to the ancient Egyptians, and so the Scarab became associated with creativity. Scarab amulets inscribed with spells were often placed over the hearts of the dead and were known as "heart scarabs." Use the Scarab symbol to tap into your creative energy and manifest your heart's desire.

SCARAB *Ritual*

Create your own Scarab amulet to make your wishes come true. Find a stone that appeals to you and cleanse it by leaving it in a bowl of water with a sprinkling of sea salt over night. In the morning, dry the stone gently and leave it either outside or on a window ledge, where it can bathe in the rays of the sun for a few hours. Finally, take the stone and a permanent marker pen and draw the shape of the Scarab beetle on its surface. Enclose the beetle in a circle to represent its association with solar power.

Hold the amulet in both hands and say a few words to infuse it with creative energy, for example, "Scarab beetle in my hands, help me manifest my plans. Light a fire in my soul, help me reach my cherished goal." Hold the amulet when making a wish for the future, and place it beneath your pillow for inspiring dreams.

Magical Tip

Beetles might not be your favorite insect, but give them a helping hand by creating lots of insect friendly areas in your garden. By helping them out, you will be storing up positive energy for the future.

SEBA

This Egyptian symbol of a five-pointed star, a line drawing based on the starfish that used to swim in the Red Sea, was used to decorate the ceilings of temples. The symbol was associated with the sky goddess Nut, who was often pictured adorned in a flowing gown of stars. The Seba was thought to represent a door or gateway and, when surrounded by a circle, became the Duat, a symbol of the otherworld, the place where the souls of the dead descended. The Egyptians revered the solar system and had a wealth of knowledge about the night skies. They believed that the stars were sacred, basing their calendar upon them. They also believed that they were the souls of lost loved ones, making the Seba an extremely powerful symbol as it formed a bridge between this world and the afterlife.

SEBA Ritual

To speak to lost loved ones and form a connection with the spirit world, try the following. Find somewhere comfortable where you will not be disturbed. Dip the fingers of one hand into a bowl of rose water and use them to draw a five-pointed star upon your forehead. Go over the star formation three or four times, until you can almost picture it upon your skin. Close your eyes and hold the image of the star in your mind. Ask the spirit world to draw close and, if you have a lost loved one in mind, ask him or her to join you. Let any thoughts, feelings, or images come to you. When you are ready, open your eyes and do something physical, such as stretching your limbs or jogging on the spot for a minute. Keep a note of any messages or insights that come to you as they may be communications from the other side.

Magical Tip

Turn your home into a peaceful haven by surrounding yourself with images of starfish, either in pictures or on wallpaper, pillows, or fabrics.

SESEN

This beautiful symbol represents the Egyptian lotus flower. According to legend, the giant lotus flower grew at the beginning of time, rising out of the chaos to give birth to the sun. At night, the flower would return to the watery depths, to be reborn again at dawn. The lotus was sacred to the Egyptians, due to its links with the creation story. They used it in many of their healing remedies, and it was also closely associated with the goddess Isis and her resurrection. The Sesen symbol is associated with the sun, creativity, birth, and rebirth. The yellow center of the flower is thought to symbolize the sun. The Sesen is also thought to be the symbol for Upper Egypt. If you are looking for a fresh start, tap into the power of this symbol. It will help you find your true calling and embrace new opportunities.

Magical Tip

For peace of mind and to create a bright new future, spend five minutes every day meditating on the lotus flower. Imagine sitting in the center of a giant lotus and let the petals of this delicate bloom soothe your thoughts.

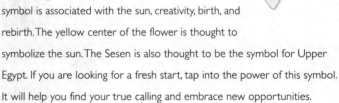

The lotus was sacred to the Egyptians, due to its links with the creation story.

SESEN *Ritual*

To manifest a positive future, try this simple ritual. Sit on the floor in a comfortable position, with your back straight and your shoulders relaxed. Place a bowl of water in front of you to represent the watery depths where the lotus grows. Light a yellow or orange candle to represent the sun and place that behind the bowl of water. Dab a few drops of water on the top of your head, in the center of your scalp. As you do this, imagine a lotus flower emerging. See it grow from the top of your head and visualize the petals slowly opening to reveal a bright, golden center. Ask for a vision or a message that will help you in the future. If you have a goal in mind, see yourself achieving it and imagine how happy and fulfilled you will feel when that happens. When you are ready, picture the petals of the flower slowly closing again and see it retreat back into your head. Use the water to rinse your hands, and blow out the candle.

URAEUS

A symbol of divine royalty and authority, the Uraeus, a type of cobra, was associated with the goddess Wadjet. One of the earliest Egyptian deities, Wadjet would often appear in the form of a cobra or as a snake-headed woman. A powerful warrior goddess, she eventually became joint protector of all Egypt—along with Nekhbet— when the lower and upper regions were unified. Due to Wadjet's status and her link with the Uraeus, it was often worn as part of Pharaohs' headdresses, making it a symbol of royalty. It either formed the crown encircling the head or was worn as an ornament on top of the head and soon became the manner by which to identify the true Pharaoh. Associated with the sun and the fiery Eye of Ra, the Uraeus was highly protective and used to empower its wearers and keep them safe from harm as it was thought that the cobra would spit venom at approaching enemies.

URAEUS *Ritual*

For a highly charged confidence boost, try this simple ritual. Take a length of red ribbon and wrap it around the base of a gold candle. Light the candle and focus on the flame. Imagine it growing in size until it fills the space in front of you. See yourself stepping into the center of the flame where it is warm and safe. Feel the bright energy filling you up, giving you strength and confidence. Say, "I am empowered and strong. I face my fears with ease!" Let your gaze fall back on the flame, repeat the magical affirmation, and then blow out the candle. Wait till the wax has cooled and then remove the red ribbon and either tie it in your hair or wrap it around your wrist as a charm for inner confidence.

Magical Tip

If you are feeling vulnerable or facing confrontation, imagine a red snake curled around your head. See it reaching out in front of you, keeping any harmful energies at bay.

WAS

This symbol of prosperity and good fortune was often inscribed into temple walls. Shaped like a rod with an animal-shaped head at its tip, it was associated with the fox-headed goddess Waset, who wore the symbol of the Was along with a feather in her headdress. She is thought to have imbued the Was with strong healing powers. Appearing in images of the deities as a scepter of power, which they would carry, copies were made and placed in tombs along with other symbols. The gods Ptah and Ra were often shown holding a Was scepter, and Osiris, god of the Dead, is sometimes pictured with this symbol, along with the Ankh. Thanks to this association, the Was is thought to represent divine dominion and heavenly powers. Radiate joy and attract an abundance of new opportunities by connecting with this symbol.

WAS *Ritual*

Create your own healing stick, inspired by the ancient Egyptian Was, with this easy ritual. Start by finding a length of wood that you can use as your stick. Gently sand down any rough edges to give the stick a smoother appearance. Create a sacred circle, using stones and crystals, and stand in the center with the stick in both hands. If you want to, you can either paint or carve a Was-type symbol into the wood or, if you prefer, you can try to visualize its presence. Hold the image in your mind and point the stick in all four directions, from the north to the east, then the south and west, in a circular motion. Say, "I bless this as my sacred Was. I raise the power in this space. I consecrate this healing stick with light and love and divine grace." Your stick is now ready for you to use either to direct healing energy at someone who is sick or to hold when you need a boost.

Magical Tip

Connect with Waset, the goddess associated with this symbol, to manifest new opportunities for growth and success. Include images of foxes around your home, along with bundles of colorful feathers.

WINGED SOLAR DISK

This ancient Egyptian symbol is associated with the god Horus, who was thought to have transformed into a Winged Solar Disk while pursuing the sun god's enemies throughout Egypt. A symbol of protection and strength, the Winged Solar Disk is often found etched into temple gates or on Egyptian seals. It was commonly believed that the heavens were two great wings that spread across the cosmos, with the sun or solar symbol at the center. Used in many different forms of magic, the Winged Solar Disk is closely associated with the element of air. If you are feeling vulnerable or insecure, the energy of the Winged Solar Disk can help you find inner strength and stability.

WINGED SOLAR DISK *Ritual*

Create a sacred pledge to protect those you love and seal it with the symbol of the Winged Solar Disk. Take a piece of paper and, at the top, sketch the symbol of the Winged Solar Disk, ensuring that the wings stretch outward to cover the width of paper. Below the symbol, in red ink, write a list of all the people and things for whom you would like to give thanks. Light a red candle and read out the list. Imagine you are making a personal request to the god Horus, asking him to keep all the things and people you hold dear in his safety. Roll up the paper into a scroll and either tie with a red ribbon or let some of the wax from the candle pool into a ball to seal the paper together. Keep it somewhere safe, such as a memory box, or on a special table or altar. You can repeat the ritual and add to the list at any point to keep the protective energy strong.

Magical Tip

For instant protection, imagine two giant wings sprouting from your shoulder blades and curling around you, like the wings of this symbol.

Going Further

If the ancient Egyptian signs and symbols appeal to you, then make a point of exploring them further. Get to grips with the Egyptian deities who featured prominently in the day-to-day rituals of the people. These gods and goddesses were user friendly and could be petitioned for help and magical assistance at any time. Most of the symbols listed here are associated with different deities, so if you want to make your rituals even more effective, get these supreme beings involved. Here is how.

- Create an altar to a specific deity and include images and effigies of the symbol you are using. Make sure you include items that are associated with this being and add to your altar every week to keep the flow of energy strong.

- Learn about ancient Egyptian traditions and practices and adapt them to suit your needs. For example, make bathing time special, as Cleopatra did, and indulge in scented oils to cleanse your body, mind, and soul while contemplating a symbol to enhance your natural beauty.

- Devote some time to meditation and take yourself on a mystical journey to the pyramids. To help, find relevant pictures in books and magazines. Imagine stepping into them and transporting yourself to ancient Egypt.

- Take inspiration from the Egyptian leaders, who would adorn themselves with jewels, amulets, and colorful charms of their favorite signs and symbols. By dressing, thinking, and walking like an ancient Egyptian, you will infuse your symbol work with potent magic.

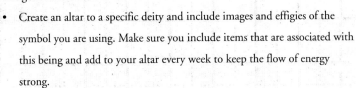

Norse Signs
& Symbols

Epic sagas and almighty battles form the basis of Norse mythology.
Based on the traditions of the Scandinavian people, Norse folklore is a
complex web of gods, heroes, mythical creatures, and worlds beyond
worlds. If you're looking for excitement and enchantment, there's plenty
here. Many of today's fantastical stories draw their inspiration from
Norse myths and legends precisely because they were strewn with such
battles for power. The Norse people had a strong belief in the afterlife
and this is evident in the carvings that adorned their burial stones, which
featured depictions of god-like figures in the otherworld. Signs and
symbols were believed to empower weapons and used as talismans to
keep their bearers safe and under the protection of the gods, and were
also thought to be connected with strength, protection, and death. Today
we can tap into this power for courage, strength, and fortitude. We can
ask the old gods to bless us with their wisdom and help us create
our own fantastical stories and adventures.

GUNGNIR

(GUNG-NEAR)

The Gungnir was the great god Odin's magical spear. It was crafted by dwarves and presented to him as a gift. He always carried the spear and, when thrown, it would never miss its mark. It became a sacred object and deemed unbreakable. Many oaths and treaties were sworn upon it. Odin used the spear to pierce his side when offering himself up as a sacrifice to the World Tree. To mark the start of the war between the Æsir and the Vanir, two different pantheons of Norse gods, Odin threw the spear over their heads. Decorated with runes of power, the Gungnir was a potent magical tool, which Odin used to craft the first set of runes. Cave drawings depict images of the god with his mighty spear, and remnants of similarly engraved spears have been found in Norse burial mounds. Use this when you want to cement a relationship or make a special promise. It will help you stay committed to your cause.

GUNGNIR *Ritual*

To strengthen a bond between yourself and a loved one, try this easy ritual. Take a knife and soak it in salt water over night. In the morning, hold the knife in both hands and offer it up to the god Odin by asking him to bless it with his power. Carve the initials of yourself and your loved one into the wax of a white candle, using the sacred knife. Light the candle and say, "By Gungnir's sacred power our bond is sealed with love. The tie that binds us, keeps us strong. Our oath blessed from above." Let the candle burn down while picturing yourself and your loved one standing together in a circle of fire.

Magical Tip

If you have your eye on someone, imagine you have a magical love spear in your hands and aim it in that person's direction. See it hit your target and bowl them over while showering them in pink light.

HELM OF AWE

The early Vikings used this symbol as part of a spell for protection and strength. It was thought that if you wore this symbol between the eyes, it would make you invincible in battle and would also strike fear into the heart of your opponent. The Helm of Awe symbol, which was often referred to as the Helm of Terror or the Countenance of Terror, comes from a type of illusion magic that was performed to control the mind. It was thought that on seeing this symbol, the mind would become confused and befuddled. The symbol was usually carved into lead and thrust between the eyes or worn as part of a helmet, so that the Helm of Awe covered the forehead. Use the magical power of this symbol when you need to feel invincible, if you're facing a challenge, or you need to charm someone.

HELM OF AWE RITUAL *Ritual*

This ritual will help you feel more confident when facing others. Although this symbol is intricate in the way it is formed, you do not have to draw it to harness its power unless you are feeling artistic. Light a black candle for strength and protection and take three or four drops of lavender essential oil, mixed with a drop of rosemary essential oil. Massage the oil in a circular motion on the spot between your eyes. As you do this, imagine a golden shield forming with the markings of the Helm of Awe upon it. See a ray of light shining from the shield, protecting you, and bathing those you come into contact with in positive energy. Know that everyone you speak to will fall under your spell.

Magical Tip

When facing a challenge, carry a piece of lead in your pocket to give you stamina and fortitude. Hold it in your hand and imagine a rod of lead running through the middle of your body, keeping you strong.

HRUNGNIR'S HEART

(HRUN-GIN-ER)

This sacred symbol was often found carved into burial stones and on weapons. A talisman against evil, it has many meanings and is associated with the god Odin and his power over death. The three interlocking triangles create a symbol with nine points, which is thought to represent the nine worlds of Norse folklore (Asgard, Vanaheim, Alfheim, Midgard, Jotunheim, Svartalfheim, Nidavellir, Niflheim, and Muspelheim). It is also closely associated with rebirth, re-incarnation, and childbirth due to the continuous nature in which the three triangles are bound together. Named after Hrungnir, the mightiest of giants who was eventually slain by the god of thunder and lightning, Thor, this is a symbol of strength, courage, and the sacred power of the otherworlds. Call on Hrungnir's heart to help you follow your heart and go with the flow in life and love.

Magical Tip

Make a dazzling first impression when meeting someone by tracing three intertwined triangles on your palm shortly before shaking hands.

HRUNGNIR'S HEART *Ritual*

To embrace destiny and discover your true calling, try this ritual. Light a white candle and place a bowl in front of it. This is for your sacred offering to the god of wisdom, Odin. Take a piece of paper and practice drawing Hrungnir's Heart in one stroke. Trace over the image nine times to represent the nine worlds and fates of Norse folklore. Place the image of Hrungnir's heart in the bowl and cover it with a piece of amber. This represents Odin's missing eye, which he sacrificed for the gifts of wisdom and foresight. Say, "Bless me with insight, a calling that's true. By the power of Hrungnir's heart, I seek that which is new." Let the candle burn down and then keep the drawing of the symbol and the piece of amber in a drawstring pouch as a charm to lead you on the right path.

JORMUNGAND

(YOUR-MUN-GAND)

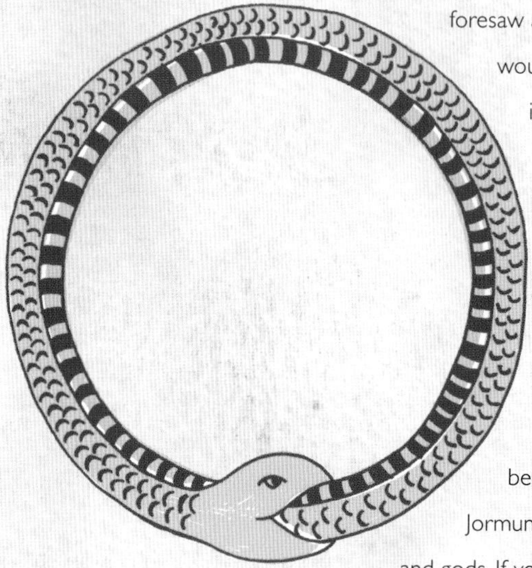

Jormungand is the serpentine son of the Norse trickster god Loki and Angrboda, the goddess of the frost. The god Odin, who foresaw a battle between Thor and Jormungand that would end in both their deaths, threw the latter into the sea in an attempt to delay the inevitable. However, Jormungand grew so big that he encircled the world in one perfect loop, earning him the name Midgard Serpent (or "earth serpent") and has since become associated with eternity and the timeless progression of the cycles of life. Considered the king of all dragons because of his almighty strength and ferocity, Jormungand's venom had the power to kill mortals and gods. If you're feeling vulnerable in any situation, the symbol of this savvy serpent will help you draw confidence and courage.

Magical Tip

To center and protect yourself in any situation, visualize a serpent, like a belt wrapped around your waist. Feel it pulling in your stomach and giving strength to your core muscles.

Jormungand grew so big that he encircled the world in one perfect loop.

JORMUNGAND *Ritual*

Try this ritual to increase strength and tenacity while working toward any goal or dream. Take a piece of black cord and wind it around your wrist; this represents the Midgard Serpent. Tie the cord and then remove and place it in a bowl of fresh water. This is particularly powerful if you can use rainwater. Place a piece of quartz crystal in the bowl with the cord and cover with a black scarf or piece of silk. Say, "Like Jormungand supports the earth, beneath the sea and ever on, the universe supports my dreams and keeps my spirit bright and strong." Leave the cord in the bowl for three days and nights to represent the three-headed nature of the serpent, then remove and wear as a bracelet to boost your vitality and determination when pursuing goals.

ODIN'S HORN

This symbol, made up of three interlocked horns, is closely associated with Odin, the father of the gods. The Horn is often seen carved into stones or worn as a talisman. Featured in Odin's quest for a magical mead, brewed from a mixture of honey and the blood of the god of wisdom, Kvasir, each horn represents a draft of the brew. Kvasir was thought to have been created from the saliva of all the other deities, which made him powerful and wise. He was killed by the dwarves, who then mixed up the enchanting elixir. Anyone who was lucky enough to take a sip would be blessed with magical skills and the gift of poetry. It took Odin three days and a lot of charm and magic to get his hands on the mead, and the horn is a symbol of his success. The interlocking horns are represented as cups and, due to the traditional association of the cup with womanhood, are therefore associated with the life-giving, feminine aspect of the divine. Use this symbol to secure your own success and to unleash your innate creativity.

ODIN'S HORN *Ritual*

To boost brainpower and intelligence, try this refreshing ritual. Collect a bowl of rainwater and fill a pitcher with it. Add in a handful of ice. Stand in the shower and raise the container above your head. Say, "Like Odin's mead a cleansing brew, this water falls with blessings, too. Prophetic gifts and wisdom clear, wash over me and bring good cheer!" As you pour the water over your head, imagine you are holding Odin's horn. Visualize the symbol in the middle of your forehead, filling you with clarity and insight about the future. You can repeat the chant and picture the symbol at any time when you need guidance or simply to clear your head.

Magical Tip

Mix a spoonful of honey with hot water and drink first thing in the morning, while asking Odin to fire up your creativity.

THOR'S HAMMER

Also known as the Mjolnir, which means "crusher," Thor's Hammer represents the Norse god's power over thunder and lightning. It never failed to hit its mark and always returned to Thor, no matter how far he threw it. It was thought to shoot bolts of lightning and could strike from any distance. In some legends it appears as an ax or club with similar powers. Carved into stone icons or jewelry, it was often found in burial cairns and could also be worn as an amulet for protection and strength. In many tales, the hammer could change its size, going from a pocket–sized charm that Thor carried easily to a mighty hammer of destruction when required. Thor's Hammer can help you break down barriers, batter obstacles, and banish negative energy.

THOR'S HAMMER *Ritual*

Try this easy ritual to overcome obstacles in your path. Take a handful of peppercorns and, using a pestle and mortar, grind them down into a powder. As you crush the pepper, imagine you are using a miniature version of Thor's Hammer. Say, "I crush and grind, my hammer strong, all obstacles in my path are gone. I banish barriers by the might of Thor, I'm ready to move forward through destiny's door." Take the remaining pepper in powdered form and sprinkle it outside while repeating the magical chant. To increase your chances of success, doodle an image of Thor's Hammer and repeat the chant whenever you need to cut through negative energy.

Magical Tip

If you have a target in mind, see it as an image. For example, a pot of gold might represent a pay rise. Take a deep breath and imagine a bolt of lightning shooting from your heart, hitting the target, and making it yours.

SLEIPNIR

(SLAYP-NEER)

Another offspring of the trickster god Loki, Sleipnir is an eight-legged horse with the ability to fly and travel through worlds. He belonged to the father of the god Odin, who used him to travel between the world of the gods and the world of matter. His eight legs, which gave him the ability to travel on land and in the air, represent the eight spokes of the solar wheel (also known as the Wheel of the Year, with each spoke representing a seasonal festival), which means he is closely associated with the sun. It is also thought that his eight legs represent the different directions on a compass. This otherworldly horse could travel faster than the speed of light and was often linked to the rays of the sun. If you need to get anywhere fast, then the symbol of Sleipnir will carry you there with ease.

SLEIPNIR'S *Ritual*

To get things moving in any area of your life, try this ritual inspired by Sleipnir. Stand outside the light of the sun. Choose a time in the day when the sun is high in the sky and at its brightest. Walk clockwise in a circle, going around eight times, and then do the same thing anti-clockwise, for another eight times. As you do this, think about all the things that you would like to achieve to move forward. Imagine watching a film in your head where you see things playing out exactly as you would like them to be. For example, if you are stuck in a job that you hate, see yourself applying for new jobs, getting invited for an interview, winning over the boss, and finally accepting the job. Ask Sleipnir to bless you with speed and swift action.

Magical Tip

Find a beautiful image of wild horses galloping and keep it on your desk or somewhere in your workplace. It will motivate you and help you climb the career ladder.

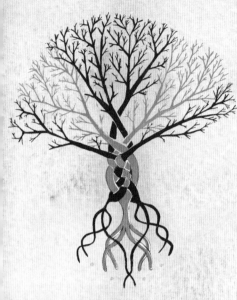

YGGDRASIL

(IG-DRUH-SIL)

This symbol represents the World Tree, a giant ash that supports the nine worlds in Norse mythology. It is guarded by the serpent Jormungand and considered highly sacred. The king of the gods, Odin, hung from the tree for nine nights to gain wisdom and secure the knowledge of the runes. The tree supported him, its roots mixing with his veins to sustain him. It is home to a number of magical creatures, including Nidhogg the Dragon, the rooster Gullinkambi, and the squirrel Ratatosk. It binds all of the worlds together, its branches extending up to the heavens. Three roots support it, one in the world of the gods, Asgard, one in the world of the frost giant, Jotunheim, and one in the misty world of the dead, Niflheim. Use this symbol's power to tap into your higher self, receive spiritual guidance, and harness inner peace.

YGGDRASIL *Ritual*

Engage all your senses and tap into your higher self with this ritual. Stand with your feet hip-width apart, preferably barefoot. Relax your shoulders and close your eyes. Take a deep breath in and imagine roots growing from the soles of each foot, reaching deep into the ground, and connecting with the roots of Yggdrasil. Continue to breathe deeply and feel the energy of the tree supporting you. Raise your arms above your head and stretch them outward like the branches of a tree. Imagine tiny threads of light extending from your fingertips, connecting you to the branches. Feel the sensation of lightness as the tree fills you with energy. Let any images come into your mind. Then relax your arms, open your eyes, and shake your limbs. Make a note of pictures or thoughts that come to you during this ritual as they could provide guidance for the future.

Magical Tip

All trees are connected to the Tree of Knowledge, so if you are seeking inspiration or you just want to still your mind, sit with your back against a tree and breathe deeply.

Going Further

If the Norse myths and legends appeal to you and you feel an affinity with the signs and symbols listed, take things a step further and do some more research. Most Norse symbols are quite angular in structure and are based on runes, so to get a real insight into their power, study the runic alphabet and what each symbol means. Try these top tips.

- Invest in a set of runes or, better still, create your own by using stones that you have collected and paint the symbols on them. Consecrate them by burying them in the earth or soaking them in fresh water overnight. Spend some time getting to know each one, holding the rune stone in your hands and letting any thoughts or images spring to mind.

- Once you have got your set of runes and you are comfortable with the signs and symbols, learn how to read them and make a point of selecting a different stone every day.

- Do some research into the folklore associated with your favorite symbols and get to know the stories in which they appear. By doing this, you will gain clearer insight into what the symbol means and how to work with it. There is a great tradition of storytelling in Norse mythology, so adopt

I would like to thank the editors, proof readers and the illustrator for coming up with some lovely images that complement the text.

a similar approach and learn to tell and share the tales with others.

By following Norse traditions in this way you'll be tapping into the creative energy of the people. This will bring you even closer to harnessing the magic of their signs and symbols.

4

Slavic Signs & Symbols

Some of the oldest and most powerful signs and symbols originate in Slavic mythology. The Slavic people had great faith and a deep respect for the deities they worshipped and a passion for the divine. They were devout and used signs and symbols as a way of expressing their beliefs. Many of the symbols mentioned here are associated with supreme beings and used in sacred ceremonies. Even today, modern Slavs have special customs and traditions that incorporate the magic of these symbols into everyday life.

AX OF PERUN

Perun was the mighty god of rain, lightning, thunder, and war. Similar to the Norse god Thor, he was renowned for his power and strength. He could shoot lightning from a bow and arrow and conjure rain to help the farmers. He was petitioned by warriors for protection and courage. His Ax, like Thor's Hammer, was used to cut down enemies, particularly evil spirits. It became an important talisman for the Slavic people, who would carve it into their own weapons to imbue them with special strength. Shaped like a battle-ax, Perun's weapon had magical properties and would return to him after each time it was thrown. If you have a personal goal or ambition in mind, the Ax of Perun can help you by creating focus and determination, and increasing your personal magnetism.

AX OF PERUN *Ritual*

Find a smooth, gray stone to represent your connection with the earth and the way it supports and nurtures you. Use a permanent marker and draw the Ax of Perun on the stone's surface. Hold the stone in both hands and ask Perun to infuse it with his power. At the beginning of every week, write a list of everything you would like to achieve. Fold the paper and place it beneath the stone charm. Say, "By the power of Perun and his Ax with mighty aim, I manifest my dreams and reach these targets that I've named!" To give your magical ritual extra "oomph," read your list morning and night and repeat the chant.

Magical Tip

Every morning, think about the day ahead. Isolate specific goals and imagine lightning shooting from the palms of each hand, lassoing your target, and pulling it toward you.

DOMOVOI

(DUH-MAH-VOY)

The word "domovoi" translates as "he of the house," and describes a friendly Slavic house spirit, usually depicted as a tiny old man. This fey being makes it his business to get involved, bringing the household good fortune, and generally looking after things, when treated with respect. If, however, you get on the wrong side of him, he can cause havoc and expose his devilish nature. He tends to live behind the hearth or stove and is rarely seen, but makes his presence felt. A shape-shifting spirit, the Domovoi can change into a different animal or member of the household. Some Slavic families still like to appease the household Domovoi by either wearing effigies or positioning them around the houses, and also by leaving food out for the little creature. Tap into his accommodating nature when you want to increase good vibrations among family and friends.

Magical Tip

For a happy home atmosphere, leave a few cookie crumbs and a small glass of milk for the Domovoi somewhere near your fireplace overnight.

DOMOVOI *Ritual*

Create an altar to invite friendly house spirits into your abode and improve relationships among family members. Take a blue tablecloth or handkerchief to cover the area. This represents the Domovoi's blue outfit. Position a vase of yellow flowers and two lumps of quartz crystal to represent his yellowing skin and bright eyes.

Finally, add a white candle on top to represent his white beard. Also leave a dish with candies or cookie crumbs as an offering. Light the candle and make a request for friendly spirits to enter your home and increase the flow of positive energy. Every day, refresh the flowers, light the candle, and ensure the spirits know that they are welcome by opening all the windows.

DOUBLE-TAILED LION

This ancient heraldic symbol of Bohemia (now incorporated into the coat of arms of the Czech Republic) has powerful significance. The lion, which is thought to be both brave and ferocious, appears with a forked tail. If the tail was lowered between his legs, it would be seen as cowardly, but because it is raised and forked, it is a positive symbol of courage and greatness. This image represents the gateway into Slavic territory. It is also associated with the story of King Bruncvik of Bohemia, who longed for excitement and adventure. He decided to leave the comfort of his throne behind and travel the world. On his journey, he encountered a double-tailed lion, who became his friend and protector. The lion returned with the king, who—in honor of his loyal friend—requested that all gates in the country be painted with a two-tailed lion. Both the lion and King Bruncvik died on the same day. A symbol of courage, friendship, honor, and loyalty, the Double-Tailed Lion can be called upon to heal rifts, find your voice, and radiate love.

DOUBLE-TAILED LION *Ritual*

Use the majesty of this ancient symbol to help you speak your truth every day. Try recreating the symbol of a red Double-Tailed Lion. Take inspiration from heraldic images or, if you prefer, find a picture that you can keep. Once you have the image in front of you, spend some time thinking about the bravery of the lion in the story of King Bruncvik. Ask the lion to protect you and give you courage to express how you feel at all times. Take the picture of the lion and place it beneath your bed. Every night before you go to sleep, ask the lion to watch over you, to replenish your strength and confidence, ready for the next day.

Magical Tip

Protect loved ones and keep relationships strong—picture yourself and the object of your affection standing beneath an arched gateway with the symbol of the Double-Tailed Lion watching over you.

KOLOVRAT

(KO-LOV-RAT)

This ancient Slavic symbol translates as "spinning wheel" and represents the cycles of life, moving from birth, to death, and then rebirth. A powerful protection symbol, it is associated with the sun god Svarog, who is thought to have created the world. The Kolovrat is a symbol of movement and transition, and it represents strength. The rotating wheel suggests universal energy in full flow and is also closely associated with the sun and the element of fire. A beacon of the old faith, this symbol is thought to unite Slavic people around the world, bringing them together, and reminding them of their roots. For personal empowerment and strength over adversity, tap into the energy of the Kolovrat.

KOLOVRAT *Ritual*

To build up power and energy, try this simple ritual, which incorporates movement and visualization. Start by marching gently on the spot, increasing your speed slowly, until you have a good rhythm going. Begin to move in a clockwise motion, plotting out a circle with each step. As you march around the circle repeatedly, imagine that with every step, you are turning a wheel. See the spokes travel around, picking up speed and momentum, and taking you forward into a bright, new future. Feel the power build inside as you increase your speed. If you feel like it, go from marching to running in a circle for a couple of minutes, then gradually decrease your speed, coming back to marching on the spot. Shake your body and feel the energy flowing through your system.

Magical Tip

The sun, like the Kolovrat, is a spinning orb of pure energy. Tap into its power with a sun salute. Stretch your arms upward, then sweep them out in a circular motion and imagine the sun's rays hitting your chest.

LUNITSA

(LOON-NIT-SA)

The Lunitsa is a symbol that was often worn as a pendant by Slavic women.
Wearing it was thought to increase fertility, attract good luck, and help you live
a long and happy life. The word "lunitsa" means "little moon" and, along with
the crescent-moon shape, suggests that the symbol is associated with lunar
power. Tap into the power of this beautiful symbol to boost your creative
energy and when you are in need of nurturing or healing.

LUNITSA *Ritual*

*This simple ritual will help to focus your mind
and unlock your creative spirit. Take a large
piece of white paper and fill the page with
a huge crescent moon. Continue to trace
this shape, over and over, until you feel it is
embedded in your mind. Spend a few more
minutes looking at the shape you have drawn,
and then close your eyes. Imagine you are
gazing at a picture of the night sky and you can
see the crescent moon. Watch as the picture gets
bigger and brighter, and then see yourself stepping into it.
Imagine you are sitting on the crescent moon, taking in the
beauty of the universe. You can sense that you have the world at your feet,
that you can make all your dreams come true. Spend a few minutes enjoying this feeling and, when you
are ready, imagine stepping back out of the picture. Open your eyes and re-focus on your original
drawing. Place it somewhere prominent to remind you that you have the potential to achieve anything.*

Magical Tip

Holding or wearing a piece of moonstone
will help you connect to the power of the
Lunitsa. On the night of a clear crescent
moon, stand outside, hold the moonstone
up, and ask the moon to infuse it with
feminine power and strength.

MOKOSH

Mokosh is the divine mother goddess in Slavic lore; she tends to the earth, giving it her bountiful blessing so that it will produce crops to feed the people. A symbol of the earth's fertility, it was forbidden to spit on the ground during the spring, as Mokosh was thought to be pregnant during this time, making her a symbolic protector of women. Associated with spinning and weaving, she is otherwise known as the Spinner of the Thread of Life and responsible for weaving fate, a reason why she is also called the Mother of Good Fortune and closely associated with life and death. She provides for her people and blesses them with everything they need. In symbols, she appears as a figure carved into stone and is often depicted with a bird in each hand. Use the symbol of Mokosh to turn around your fortunes, increase prosperity, and also if you are trying to conceive.

MOKOSH *Ritual*

To attract good fortune and increase wealth, try this ritual to worship Mokosh and feed the earth. Find a patch of grass and take a handful of wild-flower seeds and sprinkle them in a circle. Take a bottle of fresh water and sprinkle this over the seeds, again in a circular motion. As you do this say, "Divine mother, giver of all things. As the earth is replenished, my good fortune it brings. As these seeds I sow, help my wealth to grow. I give thanks for your love and your blessings from above." Finish by picturing yourself happy and prosperous and hold the image in your mind for a few minutes.

Magical Tip

To increase feelings of abundance and to receive more of what you wish for, see yourself holding two birds of good fortune, one in each hand. Imagine these birds filling you with warmth and reminding you of all the blessings in your life.

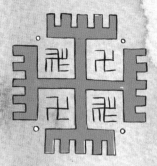

RECE BOGA

This symbol of the Slavic faith is often referred to as the Hands of God. The Rece Boga has four hands and is shaped in a cross formation. It is associated with God and the universe and was often found on old artifacts and etched into jewelry or pottery. Linked to the element of fire and the sun because of its life-enhancing properties, this energy-giving symbol captures the essence of all life. It is thought that the four hands represent the four cardinal directions, north, east, south, and west. A common symbol, the Rece Boga can be used as a general pick-me-up, for energy, protection, and strength.

Magical Tip

Infuse your morning coffee with the power of the Rece Boga. With your forefinger, trace the outline of the cross on the bottom of your cup. As you sip, imagine the symbol radiating its energy into your brew.

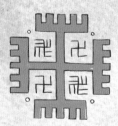

RECE BOGA *Ritual*

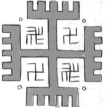

Light four candles and place them in different corners of the room to represent the four cardinal directions. Imagine a cross of fire forming between the candles, which joins together at a central point in the room. Stand in this central point where the four directions come together. Imagine being swathed in flames and feel that warm energy traveling upward from the soles of your feet until it reaches the top of your head, extending outward to the sun. Feel every part of your body filled with energy. Say, "By the power of the Rece Boga, I am revitalized. I step forward with confidence, strength, and renewed vigor!"

SVARGA

This symbol of the Slavic sun god Svarog is incredibly powerful and associated with the element of fire. Svarog was the god of blacksmithing, fire, and law, a powerful deity who liked to help his people; he would often assist with plowing the fields. He gave the Slavs the gift of fire to cook their food and an ax to defend themselves in battle. He also gave them a bowl in which to make sacred drinks and offerings, and tongs with which they could forge weapons. Due to this connection, the Svarga is a symbol that can be used to provide protection in times of trouble and to assist with solutions to practical problems. Use its dynamic energy to overcome obstacles and break bad habits.

The Svarga can be used to provide protection in times of trouble.

Magical Tip

To help you move forward in any area of life, petition the sun god Svarog by doing something practical. Take inspiration from his actions and get out in the garden and do some digging. Turn over the earth while asking for any insights to be uncovered.

SVARGA *Ritual*

Use the cleansing elements of fire and water to let go of the past with this
Svarga ritual. Draw a circle with a cross in the center to represent the symbol.
In the circle, write down anything that you would like to let go of, any bad habits
or patterns of behavior. Light a candle to represent the sun and, being very careful,
quickly pass the paper through the flame. Say, "With fire I banish you from my life."
Then plunge the paper into a bowl of water and say, "With water I am cleansed and
ready to move on." Finish by burying what remains of the paper in some soil and scattering the
water outside. Say, "By the power of the Svarga and the blessing of Svarog, I release you."

TRISKEL

Like the Celtic Triskele, this symbol, which looks like three legs joined together and is often surrounded by a circle, is associated with communication between the three levels of the Divine. It represents groups of threes that are interlinked, such as childhood, adulthood, and old age; sky, land, and sea; or past, present, and future. It's also thought to represent three states of being, for example, being awake, being asleep, and dreaming. As a result of these varied triple meanings, the symbol is associated with the cycles of life and the changing seasons. If you want to develop your spiritual side and find your true life path, working with the Triskel will help you on your way.

TRISKEL *Ritual*

Try this ritual to help you find your true calling. Take a piece of paper and sketch or copy a Triskel onto it. Along each leg write something that you enjoy doing or something that you would like to be or do. This could be something practical, such as "gardening," or something more abstract, such as "feeling fit and healthy." Look at the three things you've written and see if you can combine them in any way to create one activity that you can do and enjoy. So, for example, if you've written "gardening," "feeling fit and healthy," and "drawing," you might come up with the idea of taking a course in garden landscaping and design, which would incorporate all three things, leaving you not only fit and healthy, but also fulfilled.

Magical Tip

If you're feeling down, visualize a Ferris wheel with three spokes. Imagine sitting in the bottom carriage of the wheel and then see yourself rising up to the top where you can see for miles around. Say, "I move onward and upward to great heights."

Going Further

A deeply religious people, the ancient Slavs had strong beliefs, which are represented in many of the symbols included in this chapter. This made the symbols not only powerful, but also sacred. The people believed that each symbol had a distinct purpose and was designed to represent different aspects of their beliefs and traditions. Although there are similarities with some of the other mythologies, the core element that brings everything together is faith. To achieve deeper insight into the workings of these magical signs and symbols, try these top tips.

- Immerse yourself in Slavic history. Do some digging and look into the facts and figures. The more you discover about the ancient Slavic way of life, the more you will learn about the people's beliefs and customs and why they carried out certain practices.

- Connect with the signs and symbols on a personal level. Get creative and imagine you are a Slavic peasant and that you have to write a poem or invocation to give the symbol personal power. Then perform it as part of a ritual while visualizing your aim.

- Many of the Slavic symbols of importance are linked to the planets, in particular the sun and the moon. Try to get to know the different stages in each planet's journey. Check out moon-phases and what they represent. Say hello to the sun every morning and welcome its energy into your life. By recognizing the power of these planets, you will gain a deeper insight into why these symbols were so important.

5

Greek & Roman Signs & Symbols

The ancient Greeks and Romans were fascinated by superstition and folklore. The Romans took many of their beliefs from Greek myths and legends, and so while many of the symbols included have Greek origins, they were also commonly used by the Romans, although usually with slightly different names. Certain creatures and shapes appear often throughout Greek and Roman mythology. Great believers in magic and the mystical arts, signs and symbols were used to converse with the gods and work spells of great power. Lovers of ornate decoration and beautiful statues, they adorned their homes and palaces with these signs and symbols, so that these images were part of their everyday existence.

CADUCEUS

(CA-DU-CEUS)

The Caduceus is the magical rod of the Greek god Hermes (Mercury in the Roman pantheon). A god of commerce, communication, and travel, Hermes was fleet of foot and could charm his way in and out of any situation. The rod itself features two snakes, entwined around its length, and is topped by a pair of wings. Due to its phallic shape, it is associated with masculine energy, while the snakes are associated with feminine energy. According to ancient beliefs snake deities were mother goddesses and so associated with fertility. Thus the Caduceus symbolizes the perfect balance of the two. The Caduceus is primarily used in magical ceremonies. This is probably because Hermes was also associated with the mystical art of alchemy. If you want to explore the magical arts, or you would just like to improve your chances of success in any area of life, use the power of the Caduceus.

CADUCEUS *Ritual*

To prepare for magical work or simply to increase your personal power and charm, try this ritual. The rod is often associated with the spine and the snakes are sometimes thought to be threads of energy traveling up the spine and connecting all the chakras. Spend some time standing tall with your shoulders relaxed and your chin tilted upward. Imagine two threads of light coiling around your spine at the base and traveling upward until they emerge from the top of your skull. Feel these threads of energy connecting every part of your being. Say, "I am alive with creative energy! I manifest my future with power and ease!"

Magical Tip

Make a point and make an impression at the same time. As you speak, imagine directing a thunderbolt of energy from your own Caduceus at your audience.

CORNUCOPIA

The Cornucopia (also known as the Horn of Plenty) is often pictured as a large horn overflowing with flowers and fruit. It represents the harvest and is a sign of abundance and wealth. It is commonly associated with the great god Zeus, who was suckled by a she-goat as an infant. To honor her kindness, he took one of her horns and turned it into the Cornucopia. The Romans associated the Horn of Plenty with their goddess of abundance, Copia. It was thought that this magical horn could give the owner anything, making wishes come true, and providing them with the fruits of the land. The horn shape is thought to relate to the mother goddess, who in many mythologies appeared in the shape of a cow or goat. To make your dreams come true, increase wealth, prosperity, and success, work with this powerful symbol.

CORNUCOPIA *Ritual*

In honor of the magical Horn of Plenty and to create an atmosphere of prosperity and success, create your own Cornucopia as a centerpiece. Start by gathering together a variety of fruit and vegetables in an array of colors. Place them in a crescent-moon shape on a large plate in the center of your table. Find an assortment of brightly colored flowers and scatter them over the food display. If you have any quartz crystals or semi-precious stones, add them to the Cornucopia and finish by sprinkling a few coins and notes on top. Say, "Horn of Plenty, hear my prayer, make my table never bare. Fill my life with riches true and sweet success in all I do!" Eat the fruit and vegetables and continue to add to the display with fresh offerings every week.

Magical Tip

Manifest more wealth by visualizing a giant horn-shaped funnel in the sky. See a shower of gold coins fall from the horn and gather in a huge pile at your feet.

FASCES

(FAS-CES)

This Roman symbol of unity and justice has an ax emerging from the center. It was often carried on important occasions and thought to represent power and authority. The Fasces as a weapon could inflict a lot of pain or even kill, so it was seen as a powerful symbol that represented leadership and strength. The ax at the center was thought to symbolize the power of life over death and was also linked to the death penalty. Although there is a dark aspect to this symbol, it has strength and justice at its root and can be used in times of trouble and to help you assert yourself.

Magical Tip

Face fear by imagining that you have the Fasces at the root of your spirit. See yourself standing tall like the ax in the center, stretching upward to the heavens with grace and strength.

FASCES *Ritual*

When you are feeling vulnerable or you are nervous about something, try this grounding ritual.
Gather a bundle of sticks of roughly the same size and shape and smooth them down with some
sandpaper. Take a black ribbon or cord and tie it firmly around the sticks to secure them in place.
Hold them in both hands and imagine that you are holding the Fasces. Feel the powerful energy of this
mighty symbol traveling into your hands, up your arms, and filling your body with strength. Say, "Mighty
Fasces symbol true, through the power and strength of you, I am anchored, I stand tall, a tower of
strength, I shall not fall."

"Mighty Fasces symbol
true, through the power
and strength of you,
I am anchored, I stand
tall, a tower of strength,
I shall not fall."

KNOT OF HERCULES

This symbol, often called the marriage knot, was first used as a healing charm in ancient Egypt, but its popularity grew and the Greeks and Romans began to use it in marriage ceremonies as a protective amulet. Thought to represent the bride's virginity, the knot was worn around the girdle by the bride; it was untied by the husband on the wedding night. It is a symbol of love, unity, and marriage and represents the binding together of two people. It is also, most probably, the origin of the common phrase "tying the knot." It was called the Knot of Hercules because it was associated with this demi-god's strength and fertility. If you are looking for love, to cement an existing relationship, or you want to boost your fertility, this is the symbol with which to work.

KNOT OF HERCULES *Ritual*

If you are looking to attract new love into your life, then this simple ritual could help. Invest in a piece of braid, long enough to fit loosely around your waist. If possible, go for shades of red or pink. Infuse the braid with your intention by placing it in front of a red candle. Put a piece of rose quartz on top and say, "By the Knot of Hercules, new love I now do seize. With an open heart and mind, true love I now do find." Let the candle burn down while thinking about the kind of partner you would like to attract. Wear the braid around your waist for a few minutes every day and imagine you are surrounded by a rosy pink glow.

Magical Tip

To increase your fertility, take a rope and tie a knot in it while saying, "This knot I tie to seal a fate. A brand new life I now create!" Leave it beneath the bed for a month and let nature take its course.

LABRYS

(LA-BRYS)

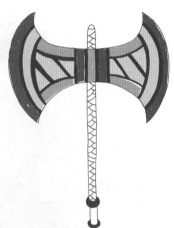

This double-headed ax, which dates back to the Minoan civilization (c. twenty-seventh century BCE–fifteenth century BCE), was popular with the ancient Greeks. It comes in all shapes and sizes, with some standing much taller than a human. The Labrys, although commonly used in carpentry, was also the weapon of choice in sacrifices to the gods and goddesses. A symbol of authority and transformation, the head of the ax appears symmetrical, like a butterfly, which suggests that this is a symbol of change. Butterflies represent metamorphosis since they shift from one state of being to another. The Labrys is most often linked to feminine power and was thought to be unstoppable in the hands of a powerful woman. Use the energy of the Labrys to increase your personal power and to help you through periods of change.

LABRYS *Ritual*

Due to its strong, feminine influence, the Labrys is also associated with the moon. Try this easy ritual that combines lunar power with feisty Labrys energy. On the night of a full moon, stand outside, place both hands together on your chest in a prayer position, and breathe deeply. Imagine that, like the Labrys, you stand tall and straight. Know that you have the power to transform your life and move in any direction. Raise your arms up and then outward to represent the two symmetrical heads of the Labrys. Say, "As one becomes two, as day becomes night, I unleash my potential and shine my light." Let your hands fall to your sides and spend a few minutes relaxing in the gentle light of the moon.

Magical Tip

Place images of butterflies around your home to promote the flow of feminine energy and help you embrace any areas of change in your life.

OMPHALOS

(AHM-FU-LAS)

The Omphalos was an important symbol for the ancient Greeks. Shaped like a beehive, this stone had a network of chains covering its surface and was used to mark the birthplace of the cosmos. The word in Greek means "navel," and it is thought to represent the very center of the world. According to legend, the god Zeus (Roman: Jupiter) sent two eagles in opposite directions around the world, with the intention that they would meet at the world's center. At this point, a number of Omphalos stones were erected. If you are looking for renewal or seeking spiritual comfort and cleansing, then work with the power of the Omphalos.

Magical Tip

To center yourself, place both hands over your navel and imagine a ball of orange light hovering there. Feel the warmth spreading across your stomach to give you a heavenly glow.

If you are looking for renewal or seeking spiritual comfort and cleansing, then work with the power of the Omphalos.

OMPHALOS *Ritual*

For instant re-invigoration, find the sacred center of your home and erect your own imaginary version of the Omphalos to mark the spot. Clear a space in your living room and imagine a shower of light coming down from the universe, hitting the top of your home, and flowing straight through the center of the room. Mark this spot by placing something circular there like a rug or a cushion. Sit on the spot and close your eyes. Imagine you are encased inside a domed shape, like the Omphalos. Feel the flow of power whizzing around you like a vortex. Feel the tingling sensation as your own body's energy field connects to this power. Spend a few minutes enjoying this revitalizing experience.

OUROBORUS

(OR-ROB-BOR-OS)

One of the oldest and most powerful symbols, the Ouroborus depicts a snake—or sometimes a dragon—eating its own tail. The word means "tail devourer" in Greek and represents eternity and a sense of completion in all things. The snake is drawn in a continuous loop, suggesting unity and wholeness, and hinting at the cyclical nature of life; hence the Ouroborus also symbolizes rebirth. In Greek mythology, it is thought that a serpent of light lives in the heavens and because of this the Ouroborus is thought to represent the Milky Way in all its glory. Some believe that the serpent was half light and half dark, giving it a sense of balance and male and female energy. Working with the Ouroborus can increase wisdom, help you connect with the cycles of life, and restore energy and enthusiasm.

OUROBORUS *Ritual*

Light a white candle to represent the cosmos and place a string of beads in a circle around the base of the candle. The beads represent the serpent of light that lives in the heavens. Spend a few minutes with your eyes closed and imagine that with every breath that you take, you absorb light and love, and that with every exhalation, you let go of negative thoughts and fears. Take the beads in both hands and say, "Serpent with your power bright, fill me with your guiding light. Bless me with your wisdom clear, help me deal with any fear!" Either wear the beads around your neck or as a bracelet for protection and spiritual guidance.

Magical Tip

For an instant lift, imagine wearing a magical serpent belt. Feel it pulling tightly on your waist and restoring your core energy.

ROD OF ASCLEPIUS

(UH-SKLEE-PEE-US)

Often confused with the Caduceus, the Rod of Asclepius is traditionally the symbol used to represent medicine. Associated with the Greek god of medicine and healing (Roman: Aesculapius), the Rod is a roughly shaped tree branch encircled by a snake. A symbol of renewal and healing, the serpent was often linked with youth and rejuvenation because of the way that it could shed its skin. A powerful healer—and son of the solar deity, Apollo (who has the same name in the Roman pantheon)—Asclepius was credited with bringing people back from the dead. Zeus, who was threatened by Asclepius's gifts, killed him with a thunderbolt. Use the Rod of Asclepius if you are in need of healing, renewal, or for personal transformation.

Magical Tip

Leave bad habits behind with this easy trick. Imagine that you can shed your skin just like the snake from Asclepius's rod. Feel the outside layer of your body fall away and imagine stepping out of it, emerging a brighter, lighter version of yourself.

ROD OF ASCLEPIUS *Ritual*

Make your own powerful healing rod with the help of Asclepius and the sun god Apollo. You may already have a staff or stick that you would like to use for this purpose, but if not, spend some time foraging in the woods or your local park. Look out for a stick or branch that is not too thick and roughly a third of your height so that it is substantial but easy to wield. To represent the snake, wind a scarf or piece of ribbon around the staff. Go for a deep blue hue to increase the flow of healing energy. At noon, when the sun is highest in the sky, take the rod outside. Hold it in both hands and offer it to the sun. Say, "With your power and your might, cleanse this rod with love and light!" Use the staff to direct healing energy by visualizing a person who is sick while holding it in both hands.

"With your power and your might, cleanse this rod with love and light!"

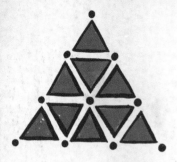

TEKTRAKTYS

(TEH-TRAK-TIS)

Tektraktys originates from the Greek word for four tetras and is a triangular figure created by the philosopher and mathematician Pythagoras. Sometimes called the mystic Tetrad, it is shaped like a pyramid and is believed to be a representation of the cosmos. Each of the ten points represents a number and is thought to explain the order in which the universe was first created. Early scholars were fascinated by the formation of the Tektraktys, making it the basis of the Tree of Life in the Kabbalah. A sacred and powerful symbol, it was highly regarded by the Pythagoreans. It signified unity in all things and the primal forces of nature. If you are looking to expand your knowledge and explore your mystical gifts, this is the symbol with which to work.

TEKTRAKTYS *Ritual*

Tap into your higher self with this pyramid ritual. Close your eyes and focus on your breathing. Imagine a picture of a pyramid in front of you. See it getting bigger until you can step inside the picture and find yourself standing at the entrance. Walk inside the pyramid, into a large, cavernous room. What do you see? You might notice certain treasures or statues. Spend some time exploring this magical place. Ask for a sign or a message from your higher self. You might receive a gift in the form of a symbol or shape, or you might see a vision. When you are ready, leave the pyramid behind and step back out of the picture. Spend a few moments focusing on your breathing and making any notes of things you have learnt or seen.

Magical Tip

For an instant memory boost, try this. If you have a list of things to recall, write them inside a triangle. Start with the first thing at the bottom and work up toward the tip, to the most important piece of information. Picture the symbol in your mind and it will help you remember everything from the list.

Going Further

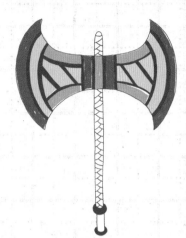

Although the ancient Greeks and Romans were lovers of all things decorative, the signs and symbols that adorned their furnishings were practical in their shape and structure. From pyramids to rods and axes, they were usually functional. To gain a deeper understanding of how and why they work, try these practical suggestions.

• Try making or working with some of the symbols suggested. Get to grips with the Double-Headed Ax or create your own healing rod or staff. The more of your energy that you put into the creation, the more powerful it will be, and you will also understand how it was used by the ancients.

• Take inspiration from both Greek and Roman decoration and introduce similar elements into your home. Go for patterned tiles, stone pillars, and statues, or scenic prints of Italy or Greece.

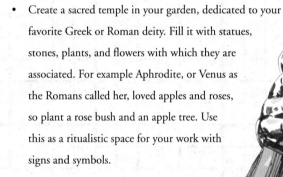

• Create a sacred temple in your garden, dedicated to your favorite Greek or Roman deity. Fill it with statues, stones, plants, and flowers with which they are associated. For example Aphrodite, or Venus as the Romans called her, loved apples and roses, so plant a rose bush and an apple tree. Use this as a ritualistic space for your work with signs and symbols.

African Signs & Symbols

Signs and symbols are part of the African way of life. African cultures offer up a rich tapestry of totem animals and symbols, which are used in ceremonies for healing both physical and emotional problems. In particular, Adinkra symbols are a popular magical tool and appear often in tribal art. Adinkra are used on cotton cloth that comes from Ghana. The cloth is stamped with signs and symbols from the Akan tribe. The symbols represent ideas, attitudes, and patterns of behavior. They also record important historical events and traditional proverbs. The word Adinkra means "goodbye," and these garments were often used in funeral ceremonies or at important spiritual and religious events. They were associated with royalty and thought of as sacred. Working with these symbols will help you find inner strength and heal yourself and others.

AKO BEN

(AKO-BEN)

This West African symbol is based on a chief's horn and is also referred to as the War Horn. It is a call to arms and represents vigilance, action, and the ability to fight for what you want or need. Originally, the War Horn would have been fashioned out of the jawbones of the war chief's enemies, the idea being that the jawbones would help to sing the battle cry and the praises of the chief. The symbol has strong summoning powers and was used to draw warriors to the battlefield. Today you can draw on its power when you need to assert yourself, stand up for something you believe in, or if you just need to get things moving in an area of your life.

AKO BEN *Ritual*

Although the Ako Ben is not a traditionally shaped horn, it's easy to draw because it looks like a crescent moon on top of some spirals. Try tracing the shape with a pin on a red candle for action and power. Anoint the candle with sunflower oil by massaging some into the wax. Light it and say, "In times of need and times of trouble, my power shines, my strength is double. By the call of the Ako Ben, I assert myself both now and then!" Let the candle burn down while visualizing a cloak of bright red light around your shoulders.

Magical Tip

Generate movement and go for your goals by developing your own war cry. Stand tall, breathe deeply, and imagine you are calling all the spirits in the heavens to your aid.

BESE SAKA

(BEH-SAY-SAH-KAH)

The Bese Saka, or Sack of Kola Nuts as it is often called, is a popular symbol of commerce in Africa. It represents abundance, wealth, and prosperity. This is because the kola nut was seen as an important cash crop and a popular treat for the people of the Akan tribes. The Bese Saka is often used as a sign of agriculture and of people working together on the land. It suggests new growth and success in all things and hints at the need to work in unity to ensure prosperity. If you are looking to increase your wealth or you are seeking career success, the energy of the Bese Saka could help you.

BESE SAKA *Ritual*

The Bese Saka looks like a flower with four petals. Invest in a stencil and create a pretty border for your walls or take a long, thin piece of gold-colored paper— to signal prosperity—and draw a row of Bese Saka symbols upon it. Use the paper to decorate your work space by either adorning your desk or placing it on the wall above. Say, "success is mine from this moment in time. Prosperity is a friend to me!"

Magical Tip

Chew a couple of kola nuts before an important meeting to fire up your senses and give you the edge. Alternatively, a couple of sips of cola—some brands' recipes are thought to contain kola nuts—can have the same effect.

CHIWARA

(CHI-WAH-RAH)

The Chiwara, often worn as a headdress, is a ritual tool used in ceremonies to represent the power of the mythical antelope. This antelope was thought to have introduced agriculture to the people of Mali. Commonly worn in ritual dances by both men and women, the Chiwara symbolizes the union of male and female energies, working in harmony. Some scholars suggest the Chiwara is actually made up of three animals, the antelope, the aardvark, and the pangolin, all merged into one. Interestingly, all three animals dig up the earth and, according to Bamabaran mythology (a Malian tribe), the Chiwara was thought to be the magical creature that taught early man how to work the land. If you need help working toward a goal or studying for something, work with the energy of the Chiwara.

Magical Tip

To increase your stamina and ability to work hard, fill your home with images of the three animals that make up the Chiwara. Read about their qualities and study any tales in folklore that highlight their magical abilities.

CHIWARA *Ritual*

Create your own Chiwara mask and infuse it with power in this easy ritual.
Choose one of the three animals that appear in the Chiwara. Practice sketching
a simple pencil drawing of the creature's face. When you feel confident, draw a full-sized
face on a piece of card. Cut out slots for eyes and decorate with colorful paint or anything
else you have to hand. Attach a pipe cleaner with tape to the bottom so that you can hold
the mask in front of your face. Light a candle and hold up the mask. Imagine, as you place it in
front of your eyes, that the power of the animal fills you with light and energy. Say, "I'm infused with
the strength and power to achieve my dreams!"

DENKYEM THE CROCODILE

(DENK-YEM)

In Ghana, Denkyem is the traditional name for the crocodile. It is also a powerful totem; healers work with its energy to become more adaptable. The crocodile is seen as a mystical creature because it spends long periods of time under water but also breathes the air, making it flexible and able to endure almost anything, being able to survive—as it does—in two different environments. People who work with Denkyem medicine are seen as strong and enigmatic, with the resilience to bounce back from hardship. If you are struggling in any area of your life and need to find the strength to overcome something, work with the energy of this symbol.

DENKYEM THE CROCODILE *Ritual*

If you are going through a bad patch and need some extra help, try this energizing ritual. Find a picture of a crocodile or, if you can, a picture of the Denkyem symbol. Place a red candle in front of it, for strength and stamina. Also place a glass of water in front of the picture. The candle and the water represent the two different environments in which the crocodile lives. Light the candle and focus on the image of the crocodile. Breathe deeply and imagine the strength of this creature filling you up. As you breathe out, picture any negative energy, thoughts, or feelings leaving your body. Slowly sip the glass of water and, with every drop, imagine that you are growing more powerful. When all the water has gone, blow out the candle and give thanks to Denkyem for his medicine.

Magical Tip

Crocodiles have tough skin to protect themselves. If you feel under attack, imagine you have the same kind of skin. Feel it hardening so that any negative thoughts or words bounce off it.

DONO THE DRUM

This hourglass-shaped drum is a popular instrument throughout West Africa. It has two drumheads, which are connected by leather cords. The drum is placed between the arm and body and squeezed to produce varying tones and pitches and is thought to be a talking drum that mimics human speech. As an Adinkra symbol, Dono the Drum represents goodwill and diplomacy. Through its link with sound and communication, it is also associated with forging bonds of friendship and teamwork. Work with this symbol when you need to improve your communication skills or want to connect with others and express how you feel.

DONO THE DRUM *Ritual*

If you have an important presentation that you need to prepare for or you just want to express yourself effectively, try this rhythmic ritual. Invest in a drum of any kind. If you cannot get your hands on one, make your own by using a barrel-shaped container and filling it with dried beans. Start by thinking about what you'd like to say. What is your message and, if you could sum it up in a word, what would that word be? For example, you might want to communicate confidence or love to a group of people. Begin by lightly tapping your drum and thinking how you would express that word through drumbeats. Let the rhythm flow and imagine you are speaking your message out loud. How would this sound? If it helps, put on some background music that fits with how you feel and tap out a percussion. Finally, picture yourself communicating successfully. See your audience, whether it is one person or a group of people, connecting with what you have to say.

Magical Tip

For an instant energy boost, stick on some African drumbeats and let the rhythm inspire you to move. Feel the beat beneath the soles of your feet, infusing you with strength and vitality.

ELEGGUA

This symbol is a representation of the Orisha Eleggua. An Orisha is an African deity and Eleggua is one of the most powerful ones. A trickster god, he is also a warrior and an opener of doorways. Travelers often petition Eleggua to help them on their way, and he is also responsible for new beginnings and opportunities. Keeper of the crossroads, he can see in all directions, making him the god of magic and mystery. He has the power to look into the past and also the future. His mercurial nature makes him flighty and he does enjoy playing tricks on people. His symbols are a red and black hooked staff and a whistle.

The Eleggua-shaped head is often crafted using cowrie shells for facial features. These heads are left near doors and doorways to welcome the protection of Eleggua into the home. They are also left as offerings in temples and sacred places. Work with this symbol and the power of its deity when you are looking for a new beginning or you need some insight into the future.

Magical Tip

To call in positive energy and open the door to an exciting opportunity, take a whistle, associated with Eleggua, and walk around your house blowing it in every room. Fling open the windows as you go and welcome in light and love.

ELEGGUA *Ritual*

Clear the path for exciting new adventures with a water ritual to Eleggua. Instead of creating your own fetish head, you can make something similar by using cowrie shells in a dish to represent an Eleggua. Place the shell dish near running water, ideally near a sink or bathtub. Take a piece of paper and write down your wishes for the future. If you are looking for a new beginning or opportunity, write this down. Place the paper in the dish beneath the cowrie shells. Start running a bath and say, "Eleggua, opener of doorways, keeper of the crossroads, clear the path for something new, help me find my calling true. Lead me onto pastures new. Eleggua, by the power of you!" Fill the bath and take a soak while repeating the chant.

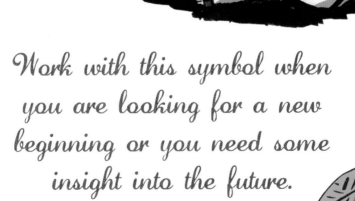

Work with this symbol when you are looking for a new beginning or you need some insight into the future.

ETHIOPIAN CROSS

The Ethiopian Cross is a powerful symbol and was first adopted by King Ezana when he converted to Christianity in the fourth century CE. Unlike European crosses, which are often quite simple in style, the Ethiopian Cross is a combination of elaborate lattice work. The cross usually has a square base, particularly if it is handmade, and this represents the Ark of the Covenant. The intertwined latticework is associated with eternal life and the divine nature of God. Often made to carry as part of a religious procession or worn around the neck as a talisman for faith and hope, Ethiopian crosses are still a popular symbol and can be used for strength over adversity and to look to the future with hope.

Magical Tip

In times of trouble, when you need hope or inspiration, make the sign of the cross over your forehead with two fingers while wishing for light and love.

ETHIOPIAN CROSS *Ritual*

To find a solution to a problem or just to ease stress, try this calming ritual. Take a large white candle to represent the spirit and dip your index finger in some lavender essential oil, which is associated with relaxation and helps clear the mind. Draw a cross on the wax of the candle with the oil. As you do this, think about anything that is bothering you or any problem that you need help with and ask for guidance. Light the candle and close your eyes. Say the following magical words: "Cross of hope and Cross of love, give me a sign from up above. Let there be light where shadows fall, let there be hope and faith for all." Keep your eyes closed and let any thoughts or images flow into your mind. Make a note of anything you see as it could prove to be a useful insight into the future.

OSRAM NE NSOROMMA

(OS-RAM-NE-SOR-OMMA)

Known as the "moon and the star," this beautiful Adinkra symbol is associated with true love, faithfulness, and harmony, which makes it a popular symbol for marriage. The star sitting on top of the moon reflects the bond shared between a man and a woman in love. There is a popular proverb linked to this symbol, which suggests that the north star, which has a deep love of marriage, is constantly waiting in the sky for the return of her husband, in this story, the moon. Use this symbol when you need to strengthen love bonds, maintain a happy relationship, or bless a union.

Magical Tip

For emotional healing, carry a piece of moonstone on a silver chain. The moonstone represents the moon and the silver chain the stars.

OSRAM NE NSOROMMA *Ritual*

This powerful love ritual is best performed at night, particularly when the moon is waxing (getting bigger in size). Take a piece of paper and write your name and your partner's name next to each other. Put a handful of white flower petals in a bowl and take them outside. First spend a few minutes burying the paper in some soil while saying, "Together we are joined in time, our love is blessed by the divine." Then scoop up the petals in your hands and scatter them in a circle beneath the light of the moon. Say, "The stars shine in the sky, casting their light and love on us!" See yourself and your loved one together and happy and hold that image in your mind.

SANKOFA

The Sankofa is an elegant Adinkra symbol that represents a need to learn from the past in order to move forward in the future. The word "Sankof," comes from three separate words: "san" which means return; "ko" which means go; and "fa" which means look, seek, and take. The idea is that you can use this symbol to return to past mistakes and learn from them. Often associated with the chief of a tribe, it suggests that he has the ability to look back into the past and to look forward into the future. It's associated with an Akan proverb, which translates as "There is nothing wrong in learning from hindsight." If you want to move forward and learn from past mistakes, this is the symbol to work with. It will help you find balance and understanding.

SANKOFA *Ritual*

The symbol of the Sankofa is often likened to a bird stretching its head back to look into the past. Try this simple ritual, which combines physical movement with mind magic. Stand with your feet hip–width apart, with your legs slightly bent. Take a deep breath in and stretch up with both arms, palms together, pointing to the sky. As you breathe out, lean backward from the waist, separating your palms and taking both arms backward. Repeat several times while thinking about an issue in the past that you'd like to learn from. When you have finished repeat this mantra: "I learn from my mistakes, I move forward with understanding and grace."

Magical Tip

The six of cups in the tarot pack, or alternatively the six of hearts in a normal pack of playing cards, are like the Sankofa. The energy of these cards is one of learning from the past to move forward. Take either of these cards and place it beneath your pillow every night to help you find peace and understanding.

Going Further

African folklore is littered with signs and symbols and wonderful, vibrant tales to explain their existence and power. If you want to gain a deeper insight into them, then spend some time immersing yourself in the colorful folk tales. Think about the meaning behind each story and how it fits with the symbol. This will help you to make the most of its power and to create effective and imaginative rituals. Here are some ideas to try.

- As you discover a tale that relates to a specific symbol, spend some time going through the story and re-living it in your mind. Imagine placing yourself in the story and how this would feel. Think about the emotions within the tale and, if you can, sum up the meaning in one word. This word represents the core message of the story and is also associated with the symbol. For example, in the story about the north star, which relates to the Osram Ne Nsoromma, you might think the core message is faithfulness as the star patiently waits for the return of the moon. Use this word in rituals to enhance the power of the symbol.

- If you cannot find tales associated with symbols, then try making one up. Have some fun and get creative. By doing this, you are opening your mind and connecting to the power of the symbol in a new and exciting way.

- Stories are made up of words, actions, and emotions. When we tell a story, we incorporate other elements, too, such as sound and images. So to immerse yourself in African cultures, play some tribal beats or include images of the landscape while re-telling the tales associated with each symbol.

7

Universal Signs & Symbols

Some symbols are universal. They are not tied to a particular mythology or culture; they are something we all understand on a subconscious level. Think for a minute about the shape of a heart—not the anatomically correct shape, but the heart that adorns cards and verses. Whether we draw it or shape it with our fingers, it is a sign of love. We are saying, "I love you." We don't need words to express how we feel because this symbol does it for us, in any language. Here are some favorites and how to work with them.

ACORN

A powerful good-luck symbol, the acorn has been used for centuries as a charm for prosperity and good health. During the Norman Conquest, soldiers would carry acorns in their pockets to protect themselves. The ancients saw falling acorns as a sign of patience and determination because they would only grow on oak trees that were fully mature. Acorns were also a symbol of strength and resilience since they would eventually grow into mighty oaks. The acorn's association with the oak tree made it especially powerful as this tree was considered sacred in many different mythologies and linked to a number of deities. In Norse mythology, the god Thor took shelter from a storm under a giant oak. Many people in Nordic countries still believe in the protective powers of the acorn and leave some on windowsills to keep harmful influences at bay. Tap into the awesome power of the acorn symbol when you need strength, good luck, or you have a particular goal for which you are aiming.

Magical Tip

Keep an acorn in your pocket or handbag when you have an important date or meeting. It will give you extra confidence and charm. Also, wearing jewelry that has been fashioned into an acorn shape will give you a magical boost.

ACORN *Ritual*

*To give you the determination to succeed, try this inspiring ritual. Find an oak tree
and sit curled up beneath its branches, as if you were a tiny acorn that has fallen
to the ground. Focus on reaching your aim and seeing yourself achieving success.
Slowly unfurl and begin to stand up with your back against the tree. Feel the energy of
the oak filling you with vitality. Stretch your spine and imagine that you are a growing tree.
Reach up your arms, and stretch your fingers to the sky. Say, either out loud or in your head,
"Each seed that I sow, like an acorn does grow. My dreams manifest, I stand tall. I am blessed!"
Spend a few minutes enjoying the invigorating power of the oak tree and, if you are lucky enough to
find any acorns scattered on the ground, pick one up to keep with you as a charm for success.*

CROSS

Although best known in its Christian context as a symbol of sacrifice, a cross has many different meanings. In pagan times, a cross was thought to represent the four elements of earth, air, fire, and water. It was also thought to signify the four cardinal directions of north, east, south, and west. These similarities were thought to suggest a physical presence and the strength and nurturing nature of the earth. Considered by the ancients as the cosmic axis of the world, a cross represents the union of the earth and the heavens and is associated with eternal life and fertility. Use the power of this symbol today when you need to find balance and strength in any area of life.

CROSS *Ritual*

If you're looking for a sense of renewal, or just to feel more grounded, try this ritual. Find a quiet spot outside and a patch of soil. With a stick, carve a cross shape into the ground. Place a piece of quartz crystal in the center of the cross, where the lines join. Say, "By the power of this axis of the earth, I seek rejuvenation and rebirth. All the elements bound into one. I am balanced and I am strong!" Spend a few minutes breathing deeply and focusing on the cross shape before you. Hold the crystal in both hands and feel yourself absorb the flow of energy into your aura.

Magical Tip

Wearing or holding a cross during times of trouble and stress can help you feel more centered and give you an inner core of special strength.

EVIL EYE

A common symbol around the world, the Evil Eye is worn as a pendant or amulet to protect against harm. The Evil Eye was first mentioned in ancient Greece and the symbol is still very popular in many Asian and European countries. It was generally used as a curse upon those who had become boastful. Any disease that could not be explained easily was thought to have come from the Evil Eye. This symbol can represent a number of things, such as a negative glance, a curse, or even a wish for someone's demise. Wearing the symbol is thought to repel evil and protect the wearer from negative influences. If you feel as if you have been cursed or you are suffering from a patch of bad luck, try working with this potent symbol.

EVIL EYE *Ritual*

The Evil Eye is one of the simplest symbols to draw. If you feel under attack in any way or you would just like to protect your home and family, try this easy ritual. Light a black candle to repel negative energy. Take lots of small squares of paper and draw an eye on each one with a thick, black marker pen. Place the eyes in a circle around the candle as it burns down. Say, "I am protected, safe from harm. We are protected, no cause for alarm. The Evil Eye repels all pain. I am free from stress and strain." Take each eye and place it under every doormat and windowsill in your home.

Magical Tip

For instant protection, quickly trace an eye symbol over your chest with your index finger. Imagine the eye opening and sending out a ray of light to repel negative energy.

HAND OF FATIMA

Also known as the Hamsa, this symbol, shaped like a right hand, is popular in Arabic and Middle Eastern countries. It is often worn as an amulet to keep harm at bay and protect the wearer from the Evil Eye. In Islam, it is called the Hand of Fatima after the prophet Muhammad's daughter. The five fingers are thought to represent the five pillars of Islam. The Hand of Fatima is one of the earliest symbols known to man. It was first used in ancient Mesopotamia as a general symbol of protection and was often worn as a charm or amulet. Some scholars believe that the hand is associated with a Middle Eastern goddess who used her hand to ward off evil. If you are feeling vulnerable and want to shield yourself from negativity, the Hand of Fatima could help.

Magical Tip

Activate your intuition when meeting someone new by spending a few minutes rubbing your palms together. Imagine a ball of bright light in the center of your right palm as you shake the person's hand.

HAND OF FATIMA *Ritual*

Create your own Hand of Fatima amulet to
protect yourself from negative influences. Light a
white candle and find a nice piece of stone,
preferably one from your own garden. Place the
stone in a bowl of salt water to cleanse it of any
residue energy and place it in front of the candle.
Spend a few minutes breathing deeply and
imagine drawing a cocoon of white energy around
you. Remove and dry the stone, then take a
permanent marker pen and draw a small, palm-
shaped hand with five digits on it. Place the stone
in front of the candle again and say, "By the
sacred power of the Hand of Fatima, I am
shielded from those who would do me harm. I am
safe, I am strong, I move forward and move on."
Place the stone in a charm bag or a piece of silk
and carry it with you at all times.

The Hand of Fatima is one
of the earliest sybmbols
known to man.

HEART

The universal symbol of love, a heart is known and recognized around the world as a representation of love and affection. Some hearts are pictured with an arrow piercing the center to suggest the first flush of romance after Cupid (Greek: Eros), god of desire and son of the love goddess Venus (Greek: Aphrodite), has taken aim. The arrow also represents vulnerability and the fact that when you fall in love, you are leaving yourself open for heartbreak. Another interpretation suggests that the heart and the arrow together symbolize a merging of male and female energy, as new bonds are formed. If you are looking for true love or you need to boost your self-esteem, then work with the energy of this bountiful symbol.

Magical Tip

To attract new love, dip your finger in some rose water and trace a heart shape over each wrist while chanting, "Love comes my way, upon this day!"

HEART *Ritual*

As the heart symbol is associated with the goddess Venus, use her powers of persuasion to increase your chances of love. Devote some space on your bedside table to Venus and make an altar to celebrate her energy. Place a single red rose in the center, a piece of rose quartz, and a heart-shaped frame with a picture of a couple looking happy and in love nearby. Every night, light a pink candle and say the following words: "My heart is open to love. I radiate love. I am surrounded by love." Imagine a rosy red heart shape in the center of your chest, throwing out soft, pink rays of light.

HORSESHOE

The horseshoe is a popular symbol of luck and protection around the world. From ancient India to Europe, it appears in environmental art and is often hung outside the front or back door. Tradition says it should be made of iron and be well worn as this shows that it has protected its wearer for some time before being used as an amulet or charm. Some countries believe that it should be placed downward so that the luck pours over you, but in the US and Britain it is more common to see it facing upward. Some scholars believe that the crescent shape represents lunar power and that it is linked to moon deities, such as the Greek goddess Artemis (Roman: Diana). In this guise it can be used as a potent amulet for protection. Work with the horseshoe when you need to turn your luck around, increase your chances of success, or to protect yourself and your belongings.

A horseshoe is often hung outside the front or back door.

Magical Tip

If you can't find a real horseshoe to hang on your door for good luck, draw one on a piece of paper and leave it beneath your front-door mat.

HORSESHOE *Ritual*

Imagine a giant golden horseshoe appearing in the sky above you and see it pointing downward above your head. Say, "Horseshoe with your golden power, on this day and on this hour, bring to me my heart's desire, my good fortune now transpire!" Then imagine a shower of gold dust pouring from the horseshoe and covering you from head to toe. If you have a specific aim or goal in mind, for example, you might want a new car, see it falling from the heavens and landing at your feet. Remember to consider how you'll feel when you have this turn of fortune and give thanks to the heavens for providing exactly what you need.

LEMNISCATE

The Lemniscate or infinity symbol, which looks like a number eight turned on its side, is a mathematical symbol that represents an infinitely large number. The symbol is considered infinite, too, in that it has no beginning or end and appears to go on forever. Throughout the world it represents time and space and the limitless possibilities of the universe. In ancient India, this symbol was associated with unity and believed to represent the balance between male and female energies. Today, working with this symbol can help bring a sense of completion and also help you tap into your higher self.

Magical Tip

Doodling the sign for infinity on a piece of paper can help when you are looking for solutions to problems. Just trace the shape repeatedly while focusing on your dilemma.

Lemniscate represents the limitless possibilities of the universe.

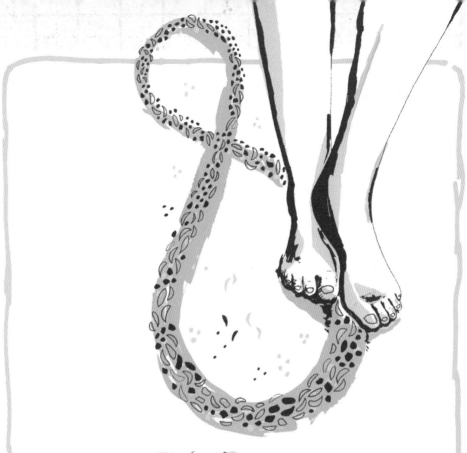

LEMNISCATE *Ritual*

To cleanse the spirit and trigger your intuitive skills, try this easy ritual. Find a quiet spot, outside or in, and mark the infinity symbol on the ground. You can either do this physically by using stones or mentally by building a picture of it in your mind. Start walking slowly around the symbol as if tracing it with your feet. After the first attempt, pick up speed and repeat until you have walked the shape eight times. With every step, try to focus on the symbol in your mind. See it as a blazing figure of eight in flames. Make a silent request to your subconscious for clarity and wisdom.

THREE- AND FOUR-LEAF CLOVER

Although traditionally it is the Four-Leaf Clover that is a popular symbol for good luck, the Three-Leaf Clover has also been used over the centuries. In ancient Greece and Rome, it was associated with the three elements of the triple goddess, the mother, maiden, and crone. The Celts believed that it was a representation of the sun. The Four-Leaf Clover also has a great deal of power; in the Middle Ages it was used as a good-luck charm and a form of protection against witches and disease. Each leaf represented a different aspect of good fortune: wealth, health, love, and fame. It was also thought to be linked to the otherworld and many people believed that if you held one in your hands, you would be able to see fairies. Today you can tap into the energy of this powerful symbol to attract good fortune, more money, and to bring a little magic into your life.

Magical Tip

For instant good luck, draw an image of a Four-Leaf Clover on the palm of your right hand. Then use this hand in all your negotiations and when buying any lottery tickets.

FOUR-LEAF CLOVER *Ritual*

It is not always easy to find a Four-Leaf Clover, but you can make your own and use it in a ritual to improve every area of your life. Trace an image of a large four-leaf clover on a piece of paper. At the top of each leaf write one of the following: wealth, health, love, glory. Beneath each of the words write something that you desire and that is associated with this area. For example, under health you might write, "I'd like to lose weight," and under love you might write, "I'd like to meet a new partner." When you have done this, repeat this rhyme: "One leaf for fame, one leaf for wealth, one for a faithful lover, and one leaf to bring glorious health!" Take the piece of paper and pin it up on a bulletin board or somewhere you are likely to see it every day. Every morning, look at the image and repeat the rhyme.

PIKORUA

Often known as the Maori Twist, this symbol, although not as well known as some of the others, is still seen all over the world. The twist, which looks a bit like a figure eight, represents the bond between two people, whether they are lovers, friends, or family. It demonstrates the path of life that we each take and how, even if we are apart for long periods of time, we are still connected. It signifies lasting love and friendship and two people coming together to forge a bond. If you are looking for love or you want to strengthen an existing relationship or friendship, this is the symbol with which to work.

PIKORUA *Ritual*

To find your soul mate, try this ritual, which combines the power of the Pikorua with some candle magic. Take a pink candle and a pin and carve the shape of the Pikorua into the wax. Splash a little rose water onto your hands and massage it into the candle while thinking about the kind of person you would like to attract into your life. Light the candle and say, "Soul mate, twin flame that burns inside. Reveal yourself from whence you hide. Our paths be joined upon this day. Soul mate be mine in every way!" Let the candle burn down while continuing to think about your future love.

Magical Tip

Make your own Pikorua love charm by bending a paperclip into the shape of the Maori twist. Hold it over your heart and make a wish for love.

Going Further

Universal symbols are easy to work with because everyone is familiar with them and acknowledges their meaning. They are literally a part of our society and we see them regularly in popular culture and our surroundings. If you want to go into more depth with your symbol work, then simply be present every day. Here are some top tips.

- Engage all your senses at all times. Whether you are out for a stroll or on your way to work, take note of your surroundings. Check out any signs or symbols that you see and consider what they mean to you. How do they make you feel when you see them?

- Compile a book of universal symbols that you can call on at any time. The beauty of these symbols is that, because they are still used today, they are often simple to visualize. This makes it easy to work with them on the run, because all you have to do is picture them in your mind and make a mental affirmation.

- Use them in everyday communication. For example, if you are writing a message, you might want to incorporate a sun sign to express your happiness. By making them a part of your language, you will gain a deeper understanding of their power.

Personal Power Symbols

Signs and symbols seep into mythologies and resonate with us on various levels—but they are also personal. It is down to personal choice which ones you feel drawn to using and how you use them. It could be because you like a particular mythology, or you just like the shape and look of the symbol. It could be that it reminds you of something from your past, or you like the folklore associated with it. The fact is that your response to the symbol is a personal one. It is about how it makes you feel. So it makes sense that if you create your own personal power symbol, something that you connect with on a higher level, then this is going to be extremely potent and could help in every area of life. With that in mind, this chapter looks at how you can identify and shape your own symbol, how to work with it in rituals and spells, and how to integrate it into everyday life.

DISCOVERING YOUR SYMBOL

Think about the symbols in this book. Have any jumped out at you and, if so, do they have anything in common? Perhaps they are a similar shape or they are made up of numbers or patterns that are the same. Maybe you are thinking of a composite of symbols, so you might have a Celtic Cross surrounded by a circle, or you might like any symbol that is shaped like the wheel of fortune.

Draw up a list of any symbols that you would like to work with and see whether you can draw comparisons among them. This will give you a good place to start with your research. Practice drawing the symbols that you like and notice how they make you feel. Are they easy to copy, do they flow continuously like the eternity symbol, or are they more angular like some of the Norse signs and symbols?

If you cannot find any signs or symbols that leap out at you, then try something different. Think about numbers and pictures that mean something to you. For example, you might like a particular countryside scene, so take a minute to visualize it in your mind. Think about the shapes that make up the picture. Is there anything in particular that dominates the view and attracts your attention? Make a note of this. By considering images that you like to look at, you will start to recognize patterns and shapes that you like and could use as a starting point for your own personal power symbol.

Do the same with your favorite number. Look at how it is made up. Copy it several times on a sheet of paper and notice how it feels to create the shape. Does it have more curved edges than straight ones and is this why it appeals to you? Perhaps the number has a deeper significance, in which case you could use it as the starting point for your symbol and build other shapes around it.

MINI VISUALIZATION *Ritual*

If you are struggling with inspiration, this mini visualization will help you tap into your higher self and recognize the shapes and symbols that feature in your subconscious.

Relax your shoulders and close your eyes. Breathe deeply and imagine that with every inhalation you are taking in light and love, and with every exhalation you are releasing any negative thoughts or feelings. Take your time and when you feel relaxed, picture a doorway in your mind. See yourself standing before it and take in every detail. It might be a carved wooden door or a gold door surrounded by jewels. It could even be the entrance to a cave or a crystal palace. This is your visualization, so have fun with it and engage your imagination. When you are ready, pass through the doorway into the chamber inside.

This space harbors your subconscious mind and all the thoughts, feelings, and images that are of importance to you. Spend some time taking in the room. How big is it? How is it decorated? Perhaps there are lots of other doors leading away from this room that will take you on magical journeys, or perhaps the room is full of pictures and memories of things that are special to you. At the far side of the room, you spot a box with a key. This box holds a symbol that is important to you and could be used as your personal power symbol or as a starting point for creating something new. Take a few minutes, unlock the box, and open it. Do not worry if you cannot see anything inside at first. It takes time and practice to tap into your higher self, and sometimes the symbol will come to you after the visualization in a dream or a flash of inspiration.

When you are ready, close the box and leave the room by the doorway. Open your eyes and spend a couple of minutes stretching and shaking your limbs. Make a note of anything that you saw in the room that you think has some meaning for you and, if you can, try to re-create the symbol that you saw on a piece of paper.

FINDING SIGNS & SYMBOLS

Here are some other ideas to help you find the signs and symbols that resonate with you:

- Invest in a pack of tarot cards and spend some time looking through the beautiful images. These cards are littered with signs and symbols and you may feel drawn to a particular card because of this. Make a list of all the shapes and patterns that you see in the cards and how they make you feel.

- Peruse art galleries to discover the type of pictures and shapes to which you are drawn. Again, consider how they make you feel. One picture with a lot of rounded shapes might make you feel happy, whereas another with many sharp corners and lines might make you feel on edge.

- Get out into the countryside and take a notebook with you. Make a note of anything that you see that you like the look of. Try drawing things that pique your interest or just see what words come to mind when you look at things.

- Think about language and words and how letters fit together to create a sound. Think about your favorite words and sounds and try to draw them.

MEANING AND SIGNIFICANCE

Once you have an idea in mind for your personal power symbol, you need to give it significance. Perhaps it already means something to you and you just want to enhance this energy. If, however, you are not sure what it means and you would like to create a specific symbol for a specific purpose, then you may need to add other layers of shape to create something unique. A personal power symbol is something that you can use all the time or just at certain periods when you have special needs or requests. You can have more than one. In fact, you can create a whole set of symbols that you can use for a range of different purposes.

As a starting point, practice drawing the symbol you have in mind. Once you have a good copy in front of you, spend a few minutes focusing on the shape. Close your eyes and bring the symbol to mind. Imagine it on a big screen in front of you. Concentrate on the symbol and nothing else. Let any thoughts or feelings float through your mind and continue to focus on the shape. When you are ready, open your eyes and record any thoughts you had. You may have developed a feeling or emotion that you now associate with your symbol. This will give you an idea of the kind of energy with which you are working. For example, if you felt hot and full of vitality, this might mean the symbol is associated with action, strength, and health. On the other hand, you might have felt emotional and loving, which would suggest that the symbol resonates love energy.

Once you have established the kind of power you are working with, you need to do something to enhance this. You might choose to work with another sign or symbol to make a different shape. If so, choose something that also works with the same energy, because this will boost the symbol's effectiveness. Experiment and see how they look together. Remember that most of the Celtic knot-work designs are separate symbols interwoven to create new shapes.

OTHER IDEAS TO UNLOCK THE HIDDEN MEANING OF YOUR SIGNS

Think about how you use color. You have the option of using different colors for different parts of the symbol you are creating. For example, if you need help asserting yourself or you want to increase your personal magnetism, you could use red. If you are creating a symbol for protection, you might want to use black, and if your symbol is to increase the flow of love and healing in your life, then you might go for pink and white.

Consider the elements associated with your symbol. Is it linked to earth, fire, water, or air? For example, if it is a protection symbol that helps to keep you strong and grounded, you might want to find a special stone and paint your symbol on it. If it is a symbol that will increase the flow of love in your life, then it is likely to be associated with water, so you could find a shell and paint the symbol on it. Think about combining the element with your symbol to boost its power.

Is your symbol associated with a specific deity? For example, if your symbol includes the shape of the crescent moon, then it could be linked to a lunar goddess, so you might want to perform a cleansing ritual upon it beneath the light of the full moon. You could also charge it with items associated with that goddess. For example, if you have chosen a symbol that is based on a Greek love charm, you might associate it with the beautiful goddess of love, Aphrodite (Roman: Venus). To infuse it with her power, you might carve it into the wax of a pink candle and light it while visualizing a shower of soft, pink light surrounding you.

WORKING WITH YOUR SYMBOL

Once you have created a symbol that you are happy with, you need to learn how to work with it. Much like the suggestions and magical tips in this book, it is up to you how you do this. Take inspiration from some of the rituals mentioned or create your own. The important thing is to do what feels right because this is your personal power symbol.

Cleansing and Charging

One of the best ways to cleanse your symbol is in a simple circle ritual, which you can perform outside or in. Start by setting out a circle using stones or crystals. The circle is your sacred space where you can raise energy and charge your symbol. Sit in the center of the circle and begin by drawing your symbol on a piece of paper. If you want, you could choose to light some candles or burn some relaxing oil, such as lavender or geranium essential oils, to create an uplifting atmosphere. Place both hands on the paper over the image and imagine pouring light and love into the symbol. Make a statement of your intention, such as, "I charge this symbol with light and love."

To charge the symbol with a specific intention—for example, to give you confidence and assist you with your goals—take the paper and around the image write words that capture the spirit of the energy you would like to raise. You might write "power," "success," and "vitality." Fold up the paper and hold it in both hands. Say, "By the power of the divine, I charge you from this moment in time. My intention set, my goal is clear. I draw this powerful energy near!" If you have lit a candle, you might like to burn the paper in the flame to seal your wish or, if you are performing the ritual outside, you could bury the paper in the earth while repeating the chant.

Creating an Altar

If you have made something physical that bears the shape of your symbol, such as a stone charm or a piece of jewelry, it is a good idea to keep it somewhere special. Create an altar to your symbol by choosing a window ledge or coffee table and filling it with items associated with your symbol. For example, if you have taken inspiration from the Celts and their knot-work designs, you might want to decorate this space with other Celtic images.

Include items that reflect the four elements of earth, air, fire, and water. You might have a candle in an associated color to represent fire, a piece of crystal to represent earth, a vase of flowers for water, and a wind chime for air.

Place a dish in the center of your altar and, for an extra power boost, surround it with quartz crystal points. Keep the points directed at the dish and place your symbol inside it overnight to charge it.

If you prefer, you might want to have a special box where you store your personal power symbol. Again, it is up to you what you put in the box. You can use it for personal wishes and requests associated with your symbol.

Making Charms and Amulets

One of the most effective ways to work with your personal power symbol is to use it as a charm or amulet. This is a token—for example a piece of jewelry—that you carry or wear and that can be used for protection or to attract certain things into your life, such as love, wealth, and happiness, among other things. Amulets tend to be used more specifically for protection and keeping negative energies at bay, while charms can be charged with different intentions.

Any kind of material can be used to make a charm or amulet, and you do not have to wear it like a pendant. Simply carrying a sacred stone with your symbol inscribed on the surface is enough to activate the power. Tin and metal make good surfaces for carving symbols, and wood is an excellent choice because it comes directly from nature. If you are going to create a charm or amulet, you need to cleanse and charge it with positive energy. You can do this by holding up the item beneath the light of the sun or moon and visualizing it bathed in a ray of light. Or, if you prefer something more elaborate, conduct a ritual using candles.

Charm Ritual

Find a quiet space and set up two candles, one white for cleansing and one black for protection. Light the candles and place your charm or amulet in between the two. Say, "Cleansed and charged, forged with light. Let the power of this symbol burn bright!"

When you are ready, pick up the charm and pass it through the smoke of the flame while saying, "Spirits of the earth, air, fire, and water, bless this charm. Keep negative energy at bay, so that all is safe from harm."

You may wish to cleanse your charm or amulet again while you are using it, especially if you are carrying it for protection. The best way to do this, without performing a ritual like the one above, is to leave it soaking in salt water overnight. Otherwise, depending on what it is made of, you could bury it in the earth overnight, which will help to eliminate negative energy.

Body Art

Some people like a more personal relationship with their symbol and choose to have it tattooed upon their skin. This is not necessary to make a connection, but if you do want an extra power boost, try drawing it upon your skin with an ink pen

that you can wash off later. There are various points upon the body, including the chakras—small energy centers—that are ideal for placing your symbol. Here is a brief guide.

Wrists

Easily accessible, wrists are the perfect choice for placing your symbol. A nerve center that calms the heart rate, imagine the symbol penetrating deeply beneath the skin as you draw. Picture white light flowing around your body, increasing energy levels and general vitality.

Palms

The center of the palms radiates energy. If you rub your hands together for a minute and then pull them apart, you will feel the magnetic pull of that energy between your palms. Placing a symbol on your palms will increase health and vitality and stimulate healing power. Imagine swirling balls of light in each hand as you draw your symbol. To reflect power and confidence, place your hands over your heart and picture yourself in a cocoon of golden light. To help friends or family who need healing, hold your hands out in front of you and imagine sending light and love in their direction.

Throat

The throat chakra, situated at the front of the lower part of the neck, governs self-expression and creativity. It is the chakra that can help you speak your truth. Although you might not want to draw your symbol with ink here, you can wear it as a pendant over the throat chakra to activate this energy or simply trace the symbol with your fingers. Turquoise is the color most associated with this chakra, so if you can combine this shade with your symbol, you will enhance its effectiveness.

Chest

The heart chakra is situated just above the center of the chest. It governs love and emotions as well as self-healing. If you want to increase the flow of love into your life or you just need to balance your emotions, trace your symbol in this space. For added effect, instead of using ink, use a little rose water, which also increases the love vibration.

Stomach

Just above the belly button, you will find the sacral chakra. This energy spot governs intuition and can help you develop psychic skills and tune into positive energy. It also helps boost self esteem when activated. If you need to increase your confidence, radiate happiness, or just improve your intuition, this is the place to draw your personal power symbol. Orange is the color most often associated with this chakra, so you could use orange ink or henna to enhance the effects.

Soles

The soles of your feet are important energy centers. They connect with the earth and help to anchor you in times of trouble. If you are looking for balance and strength, try tracing your power symbol on each sole. Once you have done this, stand barefoot, either inside or out, and imagine roots growing from each sole and extending deeply underground. Drop your weight down to your lower legs and feel the roots keeping you strong and secure. If you have an important meeting to attend or you are going on a journey, draw your symbol on both feet to help you walk tall and speak with confidence.

SYMBOL SETS

If you are feeling adventurous and have lots of ideas for different symbols, create a collection of divination stones that you can use like runes, or Ogham stones. These stones, or possibly small pieces of wood, etched with Ogham symbols from the Celtic alphabet, were originally used as a way to communicate. Each symbol had a specific meaning that developed over time so that the stones were used as a tool for prophecy and insight.

To create your own divination symbol set, either gather together a collection of stones of roughly the same size and shape or find a piece of wood that you can cut into smaller, uniform pieces. Paint the symbols on each piece and leave to dry. Wrap the set in black silk to protect it from negative energy and place a piece of quartz either on top or inside with the stones. This will enhance the magical properties of each symbol.

You could also create symbol sets in the following ways:

- Incorporate your personal power symbol into the home. Draw it on pieces of paper and leave them beneath your entrance-hall doormat or on a front step to increase the flow of positive energy into your house. Draw it on walls before painting or decorating or place it behind pictures. Draw the symbol on some paper and leave it beneath your bed for an overnight energy boost.

- Use the symbol in your cooking to improve health and vitality. If you are baking a pie, try to carve it into the pastry or, if you are stirring some soup, trace the symbol into the liquid as you go. You could even try smearing the symbol with butter on your toast.

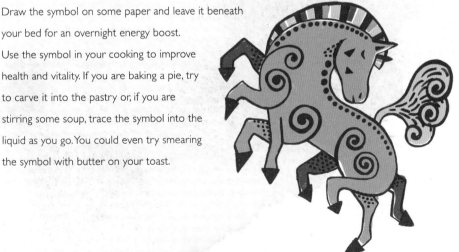

YOUR PERSONAL, POWERFUL, SYMBOLIC JOURNEY

We are a society built on signs and symbols. Our ancestors recognized their significance, assembling powerful messages around the signs and symbols they noticed in their surroundings.

They looked to Mother Nature for inspiration, and they then took this to another level, choosing shapes and signs and turning them into physical symbols that they could use in sacred rites and rituals. They and created a tapestry of tales to explain the existence of stars and planets. They looked at plants and trees and made a note of the patterns and shapes that they created, and they looked to the animal world and the strengths and habits of each creature to see how they could harness this power by working with the animal's shape in a symbolic way.

Through the mists of time, this information has grown and become almost archetypal and part of the universal unconscious. We understand just by looking at the sun that it radiates vitality and strength, and we naturally think of it as a symbol of hope and success. We understand universal symbols because they are inherent to both our specific backgrounds and also, in a wider sense, to all of humanity, and their meanings are consistent around the world. We know, for instance, when we see the sign of a cross, that it stands for something humanitarian and good, thanks to its global association with the Red Cross and, in a more western context, we also recognize its sacred nature as a symbol of the Church.

With other symbols we have to dig a little deeper and examine the specific background and culture to understand what they truly mean. For example, the swastika, in Slavic countries, used to be associated with the radiance of the sun and was a symbol of faith and hope. However, this interpretation has been misconstrued and twisted throughout history. Since the rise of Hitler and National Socialism in Europe, it has been seen as a symbol of anti-Semitism and war, but in other parts of the world it retains a different meaning. For instance, the swastika is popular in Asia, where it features in ancient artwork and was considered a symbol of prosperity and good fortune. In India some people still mark their properties with it because they believe it will bring them good luck and fertility.

Once you start looking into signs and symbols, you will begin to notice their existence everywhere. You will realize how important they are and how they feature on many levels, from the most obscure to the most common signs that we see around us. This book is a starting point—a way of learning more about the origins of signs and symbols and how to work with them.

This is a personal journey, too, and you will already have your own ideas that have formed over time, and contemplated their significance. So enjoy, explore, and, most importantly, let the magic of these ancient signs and symbols touch your life.

TEMPLATES

Use tracing paper and a hard pencil to trace your favorite signs and symbols. Reuse them on your own creations.

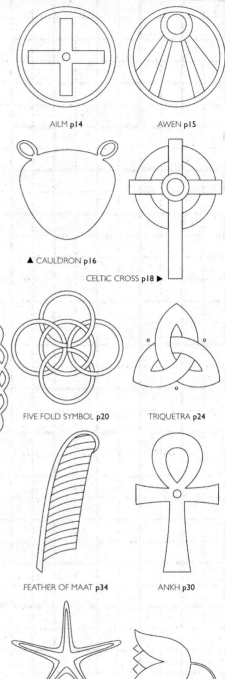

AILM **p14**

AWEN **p15**

▲ CAULDRON **p16**

CELTIC CROSS **p18** ▶

FIVE FOLD SYMBOL **p20**

TRIQUETRA **p24**

FEATHER OF MAAT **p34**

ANKH **p30**

TREE OF LIFE **p22**

TRISKELE **p26**

EYE OF HORUS **p32**

SCARAB **p36**

SEBA **p37**

SESEN **p38**

WINGED SOLAR DISK **p42**

URAEUS **p40**

WAS **p41**

GUNGNIR **p46**

YGGDRASIL **p56**

HELM OF AWE **p47**

HRUNGNIR'S HEART **p48**

JORMUNGAND **p50**

DOUBLE-TAILED LION **p62**

ODIN'S HORN **p52**

THOR'S HAMMER **p53**

SLEIPNIR **p54**

AX OF PERUN **p60**

DOMOVOI **p61**

KOLOVRAT **p64**

LUNITSA **p65**

MOKOSH **p66**

RECE BOGA **p68**

SVARGA **p70**

TRISKEL **p72**

CADUCEUS **p76**

CORNUCOPIA **p77**

FASCES **p78**

KNOT OF HERCULES **p80**

LABRYS **p81**

OMPHALOS **p82**

OUROBORUS **p84**

◀ ROD OF ASCLEPIUS **p86**

▲ TEKTRAKTYS **p88**

AKO BEN **p92**

BESE SAKA **p93**

CHIWARA **P94**

ELEGGUA **p98**

DENKYEM THE
CROCODILE p96

DONO THE DRUM p97

OSRAM NE
NSOROMMA p102

SANKOFA p104

ACORN p108

◄ CROSS p110

◄ ETHIOPIAN
CROSS
p100

EVIL EYE p111

HEART p114

HORSESHOE p116

LEMNISCATE p118

FOUR-LEAF CLOVER p120

HAND OF FATIMA p112

PIKORUA p122

INDEX

ACKNOWLEDGMENTS

I would like to say a big thank you to all the team at CICO Books for their help and hard work. In particular, I would like to thank Dawn Bates and Kristine Pidkameny, for being a joy to work with and for all their efforts in making the book a reality. I would like to thank the illustrator, Dionne Kitching, for coming up with some lovely images that complement the text.